THE EMMAUS ROAD TO MARRIAGE

THE EMMAUS ROAD TO MARRIAGE

JOSEPH D. & AUDRA A. SUTTON

Tampa, Florida

The content associated with this book is the sole work and responsibility of the author. Gatekeeper Press had no involvement in the generation of this content.

The Emmaus Road to Marriage

Published by Gatekeeper Press
7853 Gunn Hwy., Suite 209
Tampa, FL 33626
www.GatekeeperPress.com

Copyright © 2024 by Joseph D. Sutton & Audra A. Sutton
All rights reserved. Neither this book, nor any parts within it may be sold or reproduced in any form or by any electronic or mechanical means, including information storage and retrieval systems, without permission in writing from the author. The only exception is by a reviewer, who may quote short excerpts in a review.

The cover design, interior formatting, typesetting, and editorial work for this book are entirely the product of the author. Gatekeeper Press did not participate in and is not responsible for any aspect of these elements.

Library of Congress Control Number:

ISBN (paperback): 9781662961953
eISBN: 9781662957376

Dedication

This book is dedicated to the memory of our fellow pilgrims that have walked on ahead of us into the loving arms of Jesus. It is the cherished warmth of their smiles, their hugs, their presence, and their love in that time we shared that continues to fuel our passion to love others in the name of Jesus.

Contents

Introduction 1

SESSION 1: Priorities & Partnership 3
    Preparing the Way – Impact Verses 3
    Walking with Him – Teaching Points 3
    For the Road – Priorities & Partnership 6

SESSION 2: Communication & Conflict 7
    Preparing the Way – Impact Verses 7
    Walking with Him – Teaching Points 7
    For the Road – Communication & Conflict 13

SESSION 3: Spirit & Spark 15
    Preparing the Way – Impact Verses 15
    Walking with Him – Teaching Points 16
    For the Road – Spirit & Spark 22

SESSION 4: Faith & Forgiveness 23
    Preparing the Way – Impact Verses 23
    Walking with Him – Teaching Points 24
    For the Road – Faith & Forgiveness 29

SESSION 5: Leadership & Support 31
    Preparing the Way – Impact Verses 31
    Walking with Him – Teaching Points 32
    For the Road – Leadership & Support 38

SESSION 6: Pursuit & Intimacy 39
    Preparing the Way - Impact Verses 39
    Walking with Him - Teaching Points 39
    For the Road - Pursuit & Intimacy 44

SESSION 7: Privacy & Protection 45
    Preparing the Way - Impact Verses 45
    Walking with Him - Teaching Points 46
    For the Road - Privacy & Protection 49

SESSION 8: Modeling & Praise 51
    Preparing the Way - Impact Verses 51
    Walking with Him - Teaching Points 52
    For the Road - Modeling & Praise 57

SESSION 9: Projects & Work 59
    Preparing the Way - Impact Verses 59
    Walking with Him - Teaching Points 59
    For the Road - Projects & Work 63

SESSION 10: Now & Then 65
    Preparing the Way - Impact Verses 65
    Walking with Him - Teaching Points 65
    For the Road - Now & Then 70

OKAY: Now What? 71

Your Emmaus Roadmap to Marriage 73
    A Marriage Discipleship Journey (Worksheet) 73

Resources & Citations 85

Acknowledgments 87

Introduction

The purpose of this program is to help "Pilgrim" couples in their journey to develop foundational elements for their marriage before and after the "I do." Too many times in the rush and "passion" leading up to the "big day," a couple can lose sight of what God intended their marriage to become. Just as Jesus walked the road to Emmaus with two of his followers, this program is meant to help couples with their marriage journey through the discipleship and accountability of other Christian or "disciple" couples who have already been walking this road.

This ten-session program is the result of our sincere passion for couples, young and not so young, to truly live out a fulfilling marriage centered on Christ and biblical truth. Our experience has shown us that the sincere implementation of these practical points can provide a deeper and more fruitful Christ-centered marriage for those who desire to walk as one heart with Jesus by their side.

Before each session, the "Pilgrim" couple should be given the Impact Verses to look up, pray over, and discuss with each other before that upcoming session. This is meant to be an open and inclusive meeting for the two couples, where real discussion of the teaching points empowers each new step in this journey. This is not a "divide and conquer" type of guys vs gals. The sessions are designed to be done as a group of four to help foster a collective trust with an open and transparent approach. This couple-to-couple transparency creates and maintains open lines of communication and accountability as we walk this road.

We believe this program will challenge you as a couple, but we also believe Christ will be there right beside you on this road as well. Whether entering the covenant of marriage as newlyweds or celebrating a milestone anniversary, you deserve to know just how much God does truly love you. This program could be your path to a deeper relationship with Christ, and with each other. Every journey begins with that courageous first step. Courage is not the absence of fear. Courage is stepping forward anyways in the presence of fear. So be courageous, step up, step out, and take that first step—together.

PRE-SESSION 1: READY-SET-GO EXERCISE

This activity is sort of a "test" or informal measure of the "Pilgrim" couples core skills associated with a healthy Christian marriage. To get "ready" for this program, the couple's task is quite simple—"set" the table for dinner. Sounds like it should "go" easy, right? Well, it would be if you both could speak, see what you had, and move the pieces as you wish, but that's not the case.

To get "ready" you should have as much of a full table setting as possible. We suggest paper or plastic for this activity, not grandma's fine china set (things can get messy—lol). Try and get things like cups, knives, forks, spoons, large plates, dessert plates, napkins, and bowls. Before you start, mock-up a single place setting with how it should look, take a picture, and then remove those items.

What you are going to do is "set" the table for this program, by literally setting the table for the four of you. The goal is to set the table as neatly, quickly, and completely as possible in the time allotted.

There are four main rules to this activity:

1. One person is "blind," and they are the one allowed to put each of the pieces where they belong in the place settings. They are the only one allowed to touch the items on the table. An actual blindfold may be helpful here.

2. The other person is "deaf," and they are the only one allowed to "see" the actual place setting pieces during the exercise, but they are not allowed to place pieces on the table itself. Put some earplugs in if you can get some. You both are allowed to speak.

3. Both of you are allowed to touch the other person, but remember, only the "blind" person is allowed to touch the place setting items.

4. We have found that four minutes is challenging, yet possible to achieve this task in, and at the end of that time, you should take a picture of the table's final results for review later in the program.

Don't worry, this is not a pass-fail type of entrance exam. Have fun and see just how much you can get done! Your journey with Jesus starts right here, so get *ready*, the table is *set*, and it's time to *go*!

SESSION 1

Priorities & Partnership

Preparing the Way - Impact Verses

Over the next week, read the following passages. We recommend reading them at the beginning of each day so that they are kept at the top of your mind. This will help you to think and meditate on them more easily as you go about your day. Pray over them and ask God to reveal His insights on each verse.

Ephesians 5:25-26 (New International Version) "Husbands, love your wives, just as Christ loved the church and gave himself up for her to make her holy, cleansing her by the washing with water through the word."

Genesis 2:24 (NIV) "That is why a man leaves his father and mother and is united to his wife, and they become one flesh."

Luke 12:34 (NIV) "For where your treasure is, there your heart will be also."

Proverbs 27:17 (NIV) "As iron sharpens iron, so one person sharpens another."

Walking with Him - Teaching Points

Now that you've spent time in prayerful reflection on the Impact Verses, consider the following teaching points we have based on these verses.

Priorities - Budgeting You

A priority is simply whatever you apply your time, energy, money, or resources to in life. Whatever it may be, the priority anything has in your life is evident in how much of these four things you give it. Look at your life when you were around eight years old, and think of what was important to you then, and then bring your thoughts back to the present. I am sure those priorities may have changed quite a bit in that time. What are your priorities in this life you live together?

When Priorities Align

Let's take a few more moments, and each of you write down what you believe your top five priorities in life are right now. Now, no peeking, but don't think too long about this either. Take just a couple of minutes. Now let's "lay our cards on the table." What do you see? How do your priorities line up or differ? How do they compare or contrast between the two of you?

Not that every priority each of you has needs to align perfectly, but significant priorities that don't align can very well become points of struggle and division in your marriage. Understanding each other's priorities is an important tool in creating meaningful compromise and synergy in the Christ-centered marriage we seek for you.

Can I Help You?

Being a true partner also means being aware of opportunities to help the other in times of need. We all need some level of independence and personal accomplishment to function as a couple, but it is also equally, if not slightly more important, for you to offer your help to your partner as well. Help can be in many forms and many levels, but if it is never offered or never accepted, you will never know what came after the question mark.

Listen with Love

You may have heard it somewhere before that God gave us two ears and one mouth for a good reason. Why? Because He intended for us to listen much more than we ever speak. One method of developing listening skills is by practicing the principles of active listening. Active listening is intentional engagement with the other person through verbal and nonverbal cues woven into the conversation. There are a variety of web-based resources out there that are reputable and easy to understand. Sites like Wikipedia can help point out some of the key ideas and useful examples that may help us with this concept (Wikipedia, 2024). Taking a little time to deepen your understanding of what active listening is will be well worth it for this program's success.

You just need someone you trust to be present and simply listen. Listening helps you to hear, but hearing doesn't mean you listened.

KNOW YOUR WHYS TO KNOW YOU'RE WISE

While reading part of Simon Sinek's book *Find Your Why*, it became clear to us that when you better understand "why" you do something or "why" someone else does what they do, you can better process what you know and turn that knowledge into wisdom (2017). From this, we began to look deeper into our "whys," and this allowed us to better see what each of us were truly trying to say or do. Taking the time to pause and ask ourselves questions like "Why am I angry about . . . ", "Why are they anxious about . . . ", "Why are we spending so much on . . . ", and many other questions like these have allowed us to step out of our own perspective for a moment and better understand the whys behind what we do and say.

> Wisdom is **knowledge** in *action*.

A person can memorize the complete book of Proverbs, but if that knowledge is never applied to your life, then it only remains knowledge. To us, knowledge becomes wisdom when it is applied. To simply "know" something is not wisdom. We may "know" our partner needs more time to process issues than we do, and it is the giving of that time that turns that knowledge into wisdom. Wisdom is knowledge in action.

For example, a husband may know that if he treats his wife with respect and serves her with honor whenever possible, then their children can learn what it means to be a real husband and a father. The *actions* toward his wife are a display of wisdom on his part, which hopefully becomes knowledge for their children to later apply as well.

Turning our "whys" into wisdom was, unfortunately, not a priority early on in our marriage. That is not to say we didn't grow in our wisdom and respect along the way though. We have had many such "whys-into-wisdom" moments throughout our life together, but one such example that stands out to us as simple yet impactful was the act of opening the car door for Audra. The "why" was not that she couldn't open her own door or that she required that of her husband. Our "why" in that simple act was to show each other love and respect in subtle, yet public ways. We found this fun, but it also helped us to see that serving can be simple, and that allowing yourself to be served is actually a blessing to the one serving as well.

WORK THROUGH *YOUR* PROBLEMS

> **We** all want to **feel** like *we are* being **heard**, plain and simple.

It may seem like an obvious benefit to "work together through your problems," but we see this point with a little twist. When you have a problem that involves both of you, then it just makes sense that working on those problems together is the best way to work it out. For example: You are having significant problems with someone at work, and you feel like you are getting nowhere close to resolving things with them. Working on your problem *together* with your partner may just be the shift your perspective needs to see the solution.

We don't imply that you or your partner becomes the "fixer" and tells the other what to do for the problem, but they do need to be present and supportive. This points out what we believe to be a fundamental need of almost every person you see. We all want to feel like we are being heard, plain and simple. We want to know that what we think and what we feel matters.

When you engage your partner with the problems, big or small, that you are facing, you may just find out the solution was inside you the whole time.

FOR THE ROAD – PRIORITIES & PARTNERSHIP

As you consider these questions, please reference *Your Emmaus Roadmap to Marriage* so that you can capture your progress and any thoughts you may need to revisit from this session.

1. How you spend your time and money are the most telling aspects of your priorities in life. Considering that, what are your priorities?

2. What difference do you see between hearing what your partner says and listening to what your partner says?

3. Look for one or two "whys" that you can turn into wisdom with your partner. What do those look like?

SESSION 2

COMMUNICATION & CONFLICT

PREPARING THE WAY – IMPACT VERSES

Over the next week, read the following passages. We recommend reading them at the beginning of each day so that they are kept at the top of your mind. This will help you to think and meditate on them more easily as you go about your day. Pray over them, and ask God to reveal His insights on each verse.

> **James 1:19-20** (NIV) "My dear brothers and sisters, take note of this: Everyone should be quick to listen, slow to speak and slow to become angry, because human anger does not produce the righteousness that God desires."
>
> **Ecclesiastes 7:8-9** (NIV) "The end of a matter is better than its beginning, and patience is better than pride. Do not be quickly provoked in your spirit, for anger resides in the lap of fools."
>
> **Matthew 11:15** (English Standard Version) "He who has ears to hear, let him hear."
>
> **Matthew 5:9** (ESV) "Blessed are the peacemakers, for they shall be called sons of God."
>
> **Proverbs 15:1** (NIV) "A gentle answer turns away wrath, but a harsh word stirs up anger."

WALKING WITH HIM – TEACHING POINTS

Now that you've spent time in prayerful reflection on the Impact Verses, consider the following teaching points we have based on these verses.

When you Listen, You Learn

In session one, we stepped into the "wading pool" of active listening, but let's go in a little deeper. Have you tried any of those active listening concepts yet? If so, how did it go? What was difficult or easy about this communication style? If the patient and attentive approach of active listening still seems a bit foreign, then trust us in the fact that every step, big or small, toward a clearer exchange of information, thoughts, and feelings will become more natural for you both. Don't become defeated from perceived failures as you refine your active listening skills.

Don't Make the "Win" Your Why

One of the hard truths that we have learned over the years of our marriage is that when either of you focus on winning the argument, you have already lost. Why? That is because having a "fight," argument, dispute, "tiff," or whatever you call it–must be about seeking understanding and not winning. To win implies defeating your "opponent," and your partner should never be "the opposing team." So, what does "seeking to understand" look like? For us, "seeking to understand" means that we try to put ourselves in the other's position and pursue their why and what they are trying to communicate. Being respectful in our word choice, trying to see the dispute from their perspective, and trusting the other "is there for you as well" are important parts of creating understanding. Inevitably, conflict will arise, but for a couple sharing one life together, fighting to "win" means you both lose.

You Can't Expect a Rock to Not Do What a Rock Does

> An **informed** **_heart_** is able to **act** upon the **_truth_** it is given.

Unrealistic expectations only hold *you* back. Before you scratch your head too hard, imagine a nice rounded river rock sitting in your palm. Now place that rock on the ground in front of you and tell that rock to move. It is *very* likely that the rock did absolutely nothing. Why? Because that is what a rock does very well most days. It just sits there! Now, please don't look at each other and imagine your partner as some type of "dense" rock that is unwilling to move even if they seem rather hardheaded at times.

The point to this tidbit of wisdom is that looking at the rock in front of you with the expectation that it will move all on its own seems somewhat foolish and unrealistic, doesn't it? Well, we find that all too often, we all can place similar unrealistic expectations upon our partners as well. The same goes with needs or wants that go uncommunicated. Your partner cannot do things differently if they know nothing different than before. An informed heart is able to act upon the truth it is given. That doesn't mean it will, but it *can*, and that starts with openly and honestly communicating our needs to our partner!

When you have been angry with someone else, could you have been angry because they didn't do or say what *you* expected? Now, don't get it wrong, we are not saying your partner bears no responsibility or accountability in the relationship. The problem is when we do not communicate our needs to our partner, then we are the one creating our own anger and disappointment. So, the next time you think "that rock" should move, have you offered your hand to "that rock" to help show it where you need it to go?

Seeking to Understand is Not Submitting

> **Now**, do not *confuse* that when **you** "**give first**" that you are "**giving in**."

You can understand, yet still not agree! When we seek to understand, then we create room for growth in a relationship. Focusing on what the other is trying to communicate is not an act of submission, and it doesn't mean you are dismissing your needs either. As a person seeks to understand, they are humbling themself and giving their partner respect by showing that they value what their partner may be trying to say or do. Many times, we have found that when you "give" first, then you create the space for your partner to give as well. It is a form of modeling, which we will touch on in a later session. Now, do not confuse that when you "give first" that you are "giving in." Your needs are just as valid and real, but now that you may better understand what the other may be needing, you may be better able to understand your needs as well.

For example, if a husband needs his wife to not put him down in front of his work friends, and he communicates that to her, then she has the opportunity to truly understand his need for respect (not submission) when his friends are around. The same goes for her. She may be upset time and time again with him in how he consistently disregards the family's credit card budget. If he were to step back and create room for understanding the family budget with his wife, then his respect for her will likely lead to a better understanding of the needs that she has communicated as well. The point here is that respecting your partner's needs, whether public or private, is an effective place in which to give of yourself as an act of loving sacrifice and not a means of controlling each other.

Don't Just Feel Your Feelings

In our experience, it is one thing to communicate *with* feelings, and it is another to communicate *your* feelings. When having a simple conversation with your partner, there are several different types of communication going on all at the same time. These are generally broken down into verbal cues (what is said with words) and nonverbal cues (what is said without words).

In a classic example of a husband saying to his wife in a dismissive manner, "That dress looks fine, let's go!" with just a glance up from his phone, the body language, the tone of his voice, the choice of his words, and the lack of attention to her question, "How does this look?" all tell so much more than his words alone. Our communication as human beings is rarely ever conveyed with just the words we say aloud. Just his tone alone could destroy the beauty she felt just moments before. With that in mind, we have found it much more effective to try and communicate *what* our emotions are and not just let our emotions *be* the communication.

Emotions or feelings are God-given and not wrong to have, but there is a difference between feeling an emotion and being run by the emotion. Oftentimes we have seen that if we had just focused a bit more on trying to capture what we are feeling into what we say, rather than letting the feelings write the words we say, we have been less hurt and less hurtful in sensitive discussions we may have had.

Agree to Some "Safe Space"

Creating a safe space in your relationship can be helpful when dealing with issues or concerns that carry heavy emotions or deeper meaning for one of you. Especially when your partner is holding you accountable to a commitment or covenant, it may be good to agree on some key personal phrases or ways of approaching a subject that let the other know you need some "safe space." A "safe space" can be you honoring your partner by withholding judgment, keeping a calm voice, or by committing to wait for a signal to reply. A "safe space" can sometimes require a respectful amount of actual physical distance. Sometimes our emotions may need a little distance to remove the heat our physical presence creates so we can "cool down" a little easier. Stating this clearly helps create understanding in these times as well.

This "safe space" must have some level of ground rules you both commit to so trust can be established. This does not always need to be for private reasons or "bad news." We all have an internal need to feel safe with our partner. Life's journey will present many opportunities that would benefit greatly when addressed in a "safe space" where honesty and trust are maintained for each other. The beautiful thing is that the more you use your "safe space" to support your communication, the more likely those skills will seep into other areas of your life as well.

"I" Before "You" is What to Do

> ... **use** "I" **statements** **much** more than "**you**" statements.

Whenever you are trying to communicate to your partner about your needs, wants, emotions, or feelings, we have found it best to use "I" statements much more than "you" statements. In instances like these, the use of "you" statements can sound controlling or like accusations of fault to your partner. They may even put your partner on the defensive when that is not your intent at all.

You know what you are feeling or what you want, and that is best expressed as "I" statements like: "I feel safe when . . . , I need your support to . . . , I want to understand "this" better . . . , or I am confused when you say . . . . Approaching a statement you wish to make from an "I" perspective can bring greater clarity to the scope and ownership for what is being communicated. Too many times throughout our marriage, we have "blamed" the other for anger we felt by using the statement, "You are not understanding what I am trying to say!" We have found it much more effective when we say something like, "I do not feel that you understand what I am trying to say." This has provided us the room to navigate a path to better understanding what each of us truly needs.

Don't be Proud of Getting Loud

A level voice helps to ensure a level head. Conflict may arise, and shouting over the other person is never a constructive or respectful means in conflict resolution with your partner. Using the volume of your voice to combat and suppress your partner is an expression of weakness and insecurity on your part. *Frankly, yelling at your partner is foolish and cowardly–period.* If either of you feel the merit of your position is worth "fighting for," then do so fairly. You may just find out that turning down the volume of what you say may very well help you to hear what your partner is trying to say.

Don't Hurt With Hurt

There is a painful truth in the saying that "hurt people, hurt people." We had heard that years ago in a small group setting, and this is, unfortunately, very real. One way to combat that problem is never, and we mean *never* seek to intentionally hurt your partner with your words, because they may have, in some manner or form, hurt you. Yes, the truth may hurt to hear, but that is not what we are getting at. The point here is that if you find yourself stating something in an argument to make them hurt too . . . *then stop* . . . only regret and pain will result if you continue. Too many times couples choose to "hurt" the other because they feel hurt by their partner.

Intentional Follow up

We have found that there are times that a couple can help promote communication in their relationship by intentionally checking in with their partner. Having a regular check in with each other allows you to inform the other of progress or tasks on your plate, while also allowing time for your partner to do the same. The day-to-day tasks don't belong in this time. This short amount of time should be for things like the monthly bills, taxes, savings progress, or any longer-term task that one of you leads. As life works, this check in time should have some schedule to it, but leave room for impromptu sessions as well. Many times, when one of us is the primary "doer" of a family task, the other can become disconnected from that action, and some form of a check in provides a simple focus for you both to reconnect on these points. We find that our check ins have been more consistent and fruitful when we dedicated about a half hour of our time just one night of the week before going to bed to this type of intentional connection. Deeper subjects that may need more attention would likely be worked on that next day.

SESSION 2: Communication & Conflict

FOR THE ROAD – COMMUNICATION & CONFLICT

As you consider these questions, please reference *Your Emmaus Roadmap to Marriage* so that you can capture your progress and any thoughts you may need to revisit from this session.

1. Ask yourself, are there unrealistic expectations undermining our relationship? If so, what are they and where can we go from here?

2. Where in your relationship is there a need for greater understanding that could help to resolve conflict more effectively by seeking the space needed to do so?

3. Are there areas in your relationship that you can see intentional follow up benefiting your communication and understanding?

SESSION 3

SPIRIT & SPARK

PREPARING THE WAY – IMPACT VERSES

Over the next week, read the following passages. We recommend reading them at the beginning of each day so that they are kept at the top of your mind. This will help you to think and meditate on them more easily as you go about your day. Pray over them and ask God to reveal His insights on each verse.

Joshua 1:9 (NIV) "Be strong and courageous. Do not be afraid; do not be discouraged, for the LORD your God will be with you wherever you go."

2 Corinthians 3:17 (NIV) "Now the Lord is the Spirit, and where the Spirit of the Lord is, there is freedom."

Galatians 5:22-23 (NIV) "But the fruit of the Spirit is love, joy, peace, forbearance, kindness, goodness, faithfulness, gentleness, and self-control. Against such things there is no law."

Song of Songs 7:6-12 (NIV) "How beautiful you are and how pleasing, my love, with your delights! Your stature is like that of the palm, and your breasts like clusters of fruit. I said, "I will climb the palm tree; I will take hold of its fruit." May your breasts be like clusters of grapes on the vine, the fragrance of your breath like apples, and your mouth like the best wine. May the wine go straight to my beloved, flowing gently over lips and teeth. I belong to my beloved, and his desire is for me. Come, my beloved, let us go to the countryside, let us spend the night in the villages. Let us go early to the vineyards to see if the vines have budded, if their blossoms have opened, and if the pomegranates are in bloom—there I will give you my love."

Walking with Him – Teaching Points

Now that you've spent time in prayerful reflection on the Impact Verses, consider the following teaching points we have based on these verses.

Pray *WITH* Each Other

Your spirit and your spark are a unique blend of the various expressions of faith that fuel your journey together. Faith in God, faith in your partner, faith in yourself, faith in others, and faith in many other forms are key inputs to the spirit and spark you possess. The other points in this session are some of the most important ones that we have seen to support the health of our relationships.

Often overlooked, yet maybe one of the most foundational sources of spiritual fuel is when you pray *with* each other. Now, praying *for* each other is foundational as well, but there is a deeper and more intimate connection created when we actually hear the words of prayer from our partner. This is best done right there with your partner, but our dynamic lives today make this difficult at times. This is where digital means of connection help fill the gap. A video-based call or even a simple ear-to-ear phone call allows for you both to share your prayers, but this should not fully replace your in-person prayer times either. What you pray for each other is up to you, but we feel that praying *with* each other is very important to a healthy marriage.

Be Spontaneous

> **Should** we **not pursue** our **partner's heart** with no **less passion**?

When it comes to being spontaneous, we are not telling you to drain the savings and fly off on a beach vacation tomorrow. The passion of a marriage, or spark as we call it, burns a bit hotter when you can keep your partner guessing a little about what you may be doing next. Being spontaneous can look like you leaving a heartfelt note in their lunch pail, or you taking them to a movie on a Tuesday night. Spontaneous is *not* emptying the dishwasher every morning. If it is an established routine, then it really isn't spontaneous, is it?

Being spontaneous requires you to purposefully think of what creates joy for your partner and taking the initiative to act upon those opportunities. We will focus more on these later, but spontaneity is easier with an awareness of your partner's needs, coupled with the pursuit of their heart. God models this pursuit of our heart throughout the Bible. Time and time again, we see God, who is very aware of our needs, pursuing each of us out of the love He has for us. Should we not pursue our partner's heart with no less passion?

GIVE THOUGHTFUL GIFTS

Giving thoughtful gifts follows closely with being spontaneous, but what makes the giving of thoughtful gifts different and worthy of note is the silent message a personal gift sends.

Do not dismiss the impact thoughtfulness shown to your partner can have when they see that you have been listening, watching, and thinking of *them*. A thoughtful gift, in whatever form for whatever occasion, need not have a price tag, but it does create value. It means that I, the giver, spent the time and resources I had to tell you as my partner, that I value who you are and what you mean to me.

Maybe you have heard the old excuse that "It is the thought that counts!" That seems to usually accompany a gift that really didn't make sense to the receiver at the time, but there is a solid nugget of truth in there too. No, handing your spouse a $20 Visa gift card for your anniversary is *not* one of those situations where it was the "thought" that counts. That card likely says quite the opposite to them in that example.

Looking back at our session on priorities, it may be easier to see how a "thoughtful" gift is basically saying that *you*, my partner, are worthy of my time. For us, the giving of our time for each other has been priceless. We can't tell you what your time is worth, because that is unique to you two. The *time* that you invest to make that "gift" a reality is the most limited currency you have to spend. We can always earn more money, but in this life, there is no way to earn more time. How are *you* telling your partner they are worthy of your time?

READ THE BIBLE *TOGETHER*

One of the most critically important tools to develop and sustain our faith in Jesus Christ is found in reading the Bible. So wouldn't it stand to reason that reading the Bible with or to your partner could strengthen and grow your relationship with each other as well? For some of us, reading is "not our thing," so audio Bibles and various smartphone apps are valuable aids in removing the barriers we may face in reading the Bible together.

Sometimes the passages or stories contained in the Bible are fairly clear on their life application, but many times we have found that having a "study Bible" version of the translation you prefer can offer deeper insight and context to help you understand. A particular passage may strike one of you differently, and that is okay. Treating your reading of the Bible as a "check-off" list that must entail so many chapters or verses is not the type of reading we are suggesting here. Yes, you can have a target, but we caution you against creating a sense of failure by not reading a certain amount in a set amount of time. Too many people read the Bible for the participation trophy and not the eternal reward. If something doesn't make sense, then slow down and seek a reputable source to help you better understand what is being read.

Always Kiss Good night

> **Don't** let **"the drift"** deceive; **lean in** for that **kiss**.

The delicate friction of a kiss just may be the spark your spirit needs to reconnect with the one who lights your fire. So many times in our lives, we have seen the noise and distraction of the day create a small amount of distance between us. This is not really any type of anger or hurt, but the evil one is more than willing to play the long game when it comes to separating us from the love of God—and each other. We call this small bit of separation "the drift." The drift can be ever so slight. Many times, it can go unnoticed and dismissed, as "It is what it is!" or "God's got this!"

Even an inchworm can finish a marathon, given enough time. When given enough time, "the drift" leaves room for more and more of "the world" to wedge its way between the two of you. The way to fight "the drift" is to lean back in that little bit that was lost. Take a moment and imagine leaning in that last little bit before "the sparks do fly." Your partner is worth the moments it may cost to cross that distance a kiss would need. This action need not be grand. An actual kiss (which is highly recommended) or even a gentle hug helps to reconnect across "the drift" a day may create between the both of you.

In truth, a literal kiss good night is a purposeful step toward your partner's heart. Try this: Make eye contact as you draw close for that lip contact. Tell your partner, "I see *you*!" in those moments. We all need to feel seen so much more than we may say, and the same goes for the connection of our souls. We all need to feel the connection of our souls so much more than we may say as well. Don't let "the drift" deceive; lean in for that kiss.

Learn How They Love

If possible or practical, borrow or buy a copy of *The 5 Love Languages*, by Gary Chapman, and read through that book with your partner. The simple and direct purpose of this point is that it is way too easy to assume we know how our partner needs to hear "I love you" from us. Is their love language best spoken as words of affirmation, or do acts of service best say "I love you"? We have found that there is a primary or most effective means, but many times the events and situation may be better suited to one of the other general areas of love language that speak to your partner's heart.

Say *I Love You* as Often as You Can

Yes, there may be one love language you have discovered (or already knew) that may be most effective in communicating your love to your partner, but also keep in mind that the simple words "I love *you*" should be stated as often as possible as well. We are never promised tomorrow, and please don't take this as fearmongering, but many of us have suffered deep and sudden loss of people very important in our lives. It is in those times of unexpected loss that we will beat ourselves up over and over again, not being able to tell them "I love you" that one last time.

We are not perfect in the application, but in our family, we close out a day with the simple phrase "I love you, good night, and God bless you." Most every phone call or video chat is finished with at least a quick but sincere "I love you." Time yourself on how many seconds it takes you to say those three simple words to your partner. One second, yes, one single second of the 86,400 seconds you have each day is all it would cost you to tell your partner in this life, "I love you."

What if you made the effort to tell your partner you love them 50, 90, or even 120 times that day? Time is one of the most valuable resources you can spend on the priorities in your life (look back at the session one teaching points if you need to). Yes, God should always be your number one priority in life, but is not the person walking this "Emmaus

Road to Marriage" with you worthy of spending two small minutes of your day telling them, "I love you"? As for me and my house, our answer is a resounding *yes*! What's yours?

THE GIFT OF INTIMACY

Intimacy, or the s-e-x word, is a beautiful part of God's design for marriage. This teaching point is not focused on the dos, don'ts, abstinence, or even the prohibition of premarital s-e-x. We will address all of those subjects with one simple point. Our position is that any physical intimacy before the commitment of marriage is a risk to the depth of intimacy God intended for a married couple to enjoy. That is not a statement of judgment or condemnation, but a sincere point based on the observations we have made over time.

We have found that the amount of intimacy and passion a couple can share with one another is impacted the most by the perspective in which the intimacy is approached. Viewing sexual intimacy as a *gift* of yourself for your partner rather than something you can *get* from your partner is a fundamental key to achieving a depth of intimacy that is even greater than you may imagine. This is not a gift to create obligation either. To give freely of oneself without expectation or implied obligation creates the safe space a marriage needs to possess for intimacy to thrive.

There are so many challenges the intimacy of today's marriages face, especially one centered on Christ. All too often, we have heard about so many women who feel insecure in their bodies, and thus insecure in sex. Then we hear just as many problems with intimacy seem to stem from the man who initiates sex "all the time." We hate to break it to you, ladies, but men are just as fragile and insecure about themselves as well. We have found that men seem to seek "quantity" because of their own insecurity with their "quality," while a woman doubts her "quality," which often leads to resentment of "quantity." There is no easy answer here, friends, but what we do know is that honest discussion rooted in shared trust is the place you need to start.

We believe sex in a marriage is important because it is an intentional and beautiful aspect of God's plan for marriage. But why is sex important? Consider this: It was God who created woman for man and man for woman. As His creation, you were intricately designed to share yourself with your partner as husband and wife to become one flesh in marriage. For us, becoming one flesh means the joining of your bodies through sex, but we also feel God makes us "one flesh" through the children created from that very same blessing as well. The world, and especially children, will always compete for the limited time parents will share. Children are a blessing from God, and so is sex. To answer the question "Why is sex important?" we point to our belief that God designed marriage to be of one flesh, and it is through the giving of yourselves to each other to become one flesh that you will discover the beauty of God's design for your marriage as well.

How is Your Spirit?

This is a question that looks beyond the generic "How are you doing?" type of greeting. The purpose behind this question is to gently press past the empty one-word answers of "Good" or "Okay." Asking "How is your spirit?" of your partner is not meant to be an everyday type of question. We feel that this question should be asked of each other no less than monthly, but we would recommend at least weekly.

When asking "How is your spirit?" you are not seeking single-subject responses. This question focuses more on God's connection to their physical, mental, and social wellness. "How are you doing?" gives too easy of a passive exit for your partner to hide the truth of how they may be feeling. With a focus on their spirit, you are opening the scope to reflection for your partner to evaluate and respond to you with. When asking "How are you doing?" the evaluation your partner is making is likely based on a limited view of the present circumstances.

Be patient in the silence! Ask the question and then "be still." Allow their internal discussion to take place so that a genuine answer is given. This is an excellent time in which to utilize the tools of active listening that we discussed back in Session 1. It is also important to consider the timing and environment in which you pursue this subject. Walking through the door after work and blurting out, "How's your spirit, sweetheart?" is not the best choice. During the chaos of fixing supper or while watching a movie are not good times or places in which to broach this question either. Times like at the end of dinner, or just before bedtime, or even while one of you is taking a shower are opportune times in which you can dedicate intentional focus on this question. Who knows, a few "sparks" may even begin to fly as the two of you share your spirit with each other.

Overall, the scope of a question like this is to see how your partner is doing as a whole and not just how they are feeling in that moment. This helps both of you to cultivate trust and openness while also sharing the burdens and blessings of your journey.

FOR THE ROAD - SPIRIT & SPARK

As you consider these questions, please reference *Your Emmaus Roadmap to Marriage* so that you can capture your progress and any thoughts you may need to revisit from this session.

1. Do the two of you pray and read the Bible together? If so, does it seem to be working well? If not, are there opportunities to do so now?

2. How do you say "I love you" to your partner presently? Is there a need or room for change? If so, what could that look like?

3. Physical intimacy can be a "touchy subject" (pun intended). Considering God's design for marriage, where may there be some room for a bit more "spark" in your marriage?

SESSION 4

Faith & Forgiveness

Preparing the Way - Impact Verses

Over the next week, read the following passages. We recommend reading them at the beginning of each day so that they are kept at the top of your mind. This will help you to think and meditate on them more easily as you go about your day. Pray over them and ask God to reveal His insights on each verse.

1 Peter 4:8 (NIV) "Above all, love each other deeply, because love covers over a multitude of sins."

Ephesians 4:13 (NIV) "Until we all reach unity in the faith and in the knowledge of the Son of God and become mature, attaining to the whole measure of the fullness of Christ."

Ephesians 4:32 (NIV) "Be kind and compassionate to one another, forgiving each other, just as in Christ God forgave you."

Matthew 18:21-22 (NIV) "Then Peter came to Jesus and asked, Lord, how many times shall I forgive my brother or sister who sins against me? Up to seven times? Jesus answered, "I tell you, not seven times, but seventy-seven times."

Ephesians 4:26 (NIV) "In your anger do not sin. Do not let the sun go down while you are still angry."

WALKING WITH HIM – TEACHING POINTS

Now that you've spent time in prayerful reflection on the Impact Verses, consider the following teaching points we have based on these verses.

Work *Together* Through Your Problems

Most every team that exists deals with problems they are to solve as a team, and marriage is one such team. What we mean with this point is that many times in your marriage, one or the other will face life events or problems specific to that person. In cases like this, you need to be present and available to support your partner in these times. In many ways, you will not be able to really do much at all, but all too many times (even as a married couple) we try to convince ourselves that we are all alone in our struggle. Be intentional about your availability to support each other.

Many of the "we," us," or "I" problems the two of you may face will have some amount of common ground for you to stand together on, but there will also be times when there doesn't seem to be a path forward that you both can agree on. We have found in these times that stepping away from the problem for a short amount of time can help you see different perspectives, which may help to shine light on new routes of compromise and solutions. At times you may find that the problem you are facing together is just too big to wrap your collective head around.

> ***Advice*** without the ***request*** is simply you **telling** them what to **do**.

There are two routes we have found that work for us in situations that seem too big at the moment. The first route is to simplify your focus on the "here and now." If you can't seem to see the whole solution, then try to solve the parts where you can see common ground. You may just find that one small victory will lead you to a new starting point. Another route we have had to use from time to time is asking for a third-party perspective. Now, be honest and up-front here. This is not a time to gather votes for your opinion either. Seeking input from a mutually respected person that you both trust can also be the boost you two need to work from. Don't let pride or just plain stubbornness get in the way of working together through the problems you may face.

Getting Fixed

The only person you need to "fix" in a relationship is *you*! If you are on the road to or through marriage with the idea that you can fix their faults as life moves along, you are setting yourself up for some definite disappointment and frequent frustration.

As we stated in the prior point about working together with your problems, a couple needs to support each other as they grow, but you can't be the driver for your partner. Granted, you may need help to navigate an issue, but ultimately only you can fix you. You may also want to keep in mind that advice is not advice when they don't ask for it. Advice without the request is simply you telling them what to do.

Laugh *with* Love

When it comes to being together, there will inevitably be moments when one of you will wear two different-colored shoes, have a chocolate chip melted into the seat of your pants, or many other types of moments that will bring out the healing waters of laughter. Yes, just after they may have slipped on a wet spot in the kitchen is *not* a good time to laugh *at* your partner, but once you both know they are okay, a little giggle can blossom into some tummy-cramping laughter shared by both of you. Laughter may not heal your "bum," but it can surely heal your heart.

Laughter can soften the edges of our pain, but laughter also helps us to relax our grip on the idea of control we so desperately cling to. Some of our most significant comedic events and bouts of laughter together have been born from the serious and stressful times we have shared. Looking for the lighter side of life can help let out the frustrations and stress that the world likes to pile on a marriage.

With laughter, the risk we run in a relationship is found in the times we laugh *at* our partner about something. Sometimes this will further embarrass our partner, and laughing at them can even push you farther apart from each other. Making a joke at your partner's expense may get brushed off a time or two, but eventually this hollows out some of the joy that laughter normally brings.

We see laughter with each other as an absolutely necessary component for a healthy relationship. Laughter is a form of letting go of our control and letting our trust in each other take the lead. By doing this, we can create a safe place for us both to walk the edge of our hurts and allow some laughter to soften our hardened hearts.

Trust in The Truth

Friends, for God to be most present in our lives, we must "Live in the truth"! We have found that so much of the trust we have built finds its origin from genuinely living in the truth. To live in the truth applies to every part of your journey together. Whenever we have denied the truth or have hidden behind the lies we let ourselves believe, we were only robbing our lives of the blessings God had intended for us to share.

Living in the truth is oftentimes the harder road to travel when our focus is on running away from our pain. The pains held in our past, the lies we are living right now, and the fear of facing our future are powerful means from which the evil one draws his power to keep our relationship from walking that Emmaus Road with Jesus.

The Bible is our ultimate guide to the truth we should live by. Lies always seem to be easier to live with because lies often hide the pain or delay the consequences we will face. Stopping yourself from living a lie will oftentimes need the truth the Bible teaches to light the way.

There are many other tools we can use to help deal with the lies we tell ourselves. Tools like therapy, counseling, accountability with a mentor (we will explore this further in a later session), prayer, advice from a pastor, and even medications. Any one of these or a blend of these tools can be the means in which a couple can prune away the lies holding you both back from walking your Emmaus Road with Jesus.

Feed Their Faith

We believe that most people who call themselves Christians would say that faith in Jesus Christ is a simple truth that is foundational in a Christ-centered marriage. There is another faith we need to have that is fundamental in a marriage, and that is faith in oneself. Many times, labeled self-confidence, the faith that is shown in oneself rarely reflects your true talents or spiritual gifts.

Feeding the faith of your partner best resembles maintaining a good flame in a woodburning stove. Too much wood all at once will snuff out the fire, just like too much over-the-top praise can snuff out your partner's confidence. Not loading enough logs in the stove will starve the flame, just like too little praise for what your partner accomplishes or achieves will starve their self-confidence as well.

Watch for opportunities to acknowledge your partner's small accomplishments or victories. Building up the self-confidence of your partner with genuine acts of love and kindness are small investments that can yield great returns in the faith your partner has in themselves.

7 X 70 Doesn't Equal Doormat

For us, we understand "fuses blow," arguments happen, tempers flare, and feelings get hurt. We are not saying that a night's sleep means we forget what may have been done or said. Jesus told the crowd around Him that one must forgive their brother, not once, not twice, not seven times if they are offended—He challenges us to forgive seven times seventy. What? No way, right?

What we believe Jesus is getting at is the fact that forgiveness is a continual process of sanctification within yourself through Christ Jesus. Offering forgiveness to someone who hurts you is important, and that must obviously include your partner. The bigger problem lies in making yourself the doormat of your own unforgiveness.

Let's face it, we all mess up and hurt the ones we love sometimes. Accountability with your partner is vital in a healthy marriage, and communication when they harm or hurt you is an important part of living in the truth. We will beat ourselves up one hundred times more than the hurt our partner may have endured. In the same manner we cannot, by intent or ignorance, condemn our partner as well.

Sorry Doesn't Cut It

When you mess up and hurt someone else, then it is best for you to say you are sorry. To say the words "*I . . . am . . . sorry*" should be a part of every apology you offer your partner or anyone else for that matter. The famous quote by St. Francis of Assisi reads, "Preach the gospel at all times and if necessary, use words." Just as preaching the gospel is best shown by living out the word of God for others to witness, more times than not it is better for your partner to see your apology and not just hear it.

"Saying" you are sorry with your actions does not mean you need to go around all hunched over with a sad "puppy dog" face until your partner isn't mad anymore. Saying you are sorry with action can look like many things, but the most important aspect of the action is that it must be sincere and relevant. Sweeping the kitchen because you didn't water the tomatoes for three days doesn't connect well. "How can I make this right?" is a good question to ask yourself when considering how best to put "I am sorry" into action.

Forgive Without Expectation

We think it is safe to say that Jesus is the perfect example of how to forgive without expectation. We all may fall well short of His example of forgiveness, but forgiveness is a foundational element of everyone's journey in Christianity. We have found that one particular aspect of making forgiveness as fruitful as possible is to do so without expectation (or without "strings" as it has also been said).

> *...Forgiveness is a **gift** we must always **refine** with wisdom.*

Forgiving your partner without expectation is not saying you give them a free pass to hurt you again and again (remember the seven times seventy point). Just as Christ forgave all of us of our sins, we cannot place uncommunicated expectations upon our partner as a prerequisite for our forgiveness. The word we added here was "uncommunicated." Forgiveness cannot be tied to some checklist you hold in your heart. Whether you are forgiving yourself or your partner, forgiveness is a gift we must always refine with wisdom.

The gift of forgiveness is important for your partner, but in many ways it is just as important to you, the giver. The chains of unforgiveness too often hold us back from the blessed and abundant life Christ desires for us to live.

Pray With Your Partner - Quality vs Quantity

The how and what of your prayers together are not the most important parts. The important part is that you pray with each other effectively and as reasonably often as possible. Establishing a routine will help you maintain this, but the danger is that establishing a routine can relegate the prayer time together to a "check the box" on the to-do list. The best-case scenario is to allow your prayer time as a couple to blend with a few of the more predictable points in your day.

Predictable times to "share a prayer" can look like when you are getting ready for bed, or at the start of a meal, or even during one of your breaks at work. These times should blend with the dynamic or spirit-inspired moments in need of prayer as well. Inspired moments like hearing of a coworker's sick child, passing by a car accident on the drive home, or even that time before a big presentation meeting are moments where you can quickly connect with each other and "share the prayer."

For us, sharing these times of prayer together invites our spirits to work in harmony with God's plan for our marriage. Marriage is a covenant with each other and with God. Through many trials and triumphs, we have come to understand how prayer is vital for our connection to God, so it stands to reason that prayer WITH each other would help us to connect as a couple as well. The key is that you need to be intentional with your partner, and "share a prayer."

Another critical area in which to "share a prayer" is with your children. Many of us may pray *for* our kids, young and old, but it is much more impactful to pray *with* them. Whether they are "yours" or not, you both should pray with them. Modeling prayer with them provides your children with their own roadmap to grow their faith as well. It is important your children understand that regardless of their age or origin, that you love them and God loves them too.

FOR THE ROAD – FAITH & FORGIVENESS

As you consider these questions, please reference *Your Emmaus Roadmap to Marriage* so that you can capture your progress and any thoughts you may need to revisit from this session.

1. Are there areas in your journey together that could benefit from "living in truth" more effectively? If so, where?
2. Forgiveness is a powerful tool for healing and growth. Is there somewhere in your relationship that could use some forgiveness?
3. Where have you seen laughter lead you back to love?

SESSION 5

LEADERSHIP & SUPPORT

PREPARING THE WAY - IMPACT VERSES

Over the next week, read the following passages. We recommend reading them at the beginning of each day so that they are kept at the top of your mind. This will help you to think and meditate on them more easily as you go about your day. Pray over them and ask God to reveal His insights on each verse.

Ecclesiastes 4:10 (NIV) "If either of them falls down, one can help the other up. But pity anyone who falls."

1 Thessalonians 5:11 (NIV) "Therefore encourage one another and build each other up, just as in fact you are doing."

Mark 10:43-45 (NIV) "Not so with you. Instead, whoever wants to become great among you must be your servant, and whoever wants to be first must be slave of all. For even the Son of Man did not come to be served, but to serve, and to give his life as a ransom for many."

Philippians 2:3-4 (NIV) "Do nothing out of selfish ambition or vain conceit. Rather, in humility value others above yourselves, not looking to your own interests but each of you to the interests of the others."

Matthew 20:25-28 (NIV) "Jesus called them together and said, "You know that the rulers of the Gentiles lord it over them, and their high officials exercise authority over them. Not so with you. Instead, whoever wants to become great among you must be your servant, and whoever wants to be first must be your slave—just as the Son of Man did not come to be served, but to serve, and to give his life as a ransom for many."

Walking with Him – Teaching Points

Now that you've spent time in prayerful reflection on the Impact Verses, consider the following teaching points we have based on these verses.

Servant Leadership

For us, and we assume most every other Christian would agree, Jesus is the best example of what genuine leadership should look like. Jesus points out several times in the Bible that to lead, one must become a servant. In servant leadership, there are six primary qualities that capture the heart of what Jesus was trying to teach us all. Those qualities being: empathy, humility, stewardship, flexibility, integrity, and resilience (Wycliffe, 2022).

For Jesus serving was leading, and the same model can work to enhance your marriage as well. Taking the approach that each of you is there to serve the other in marriage while embracing each of those qualities listed will create a relationship rooted in how Jesus leads us.

Servant leadership is a much more detailed subject than what we can cover here, so we encourage you to dig a bit deeper into reputable resources that can expand upon using servant leadership in your lives.

Carry or Carried are Both OK

> At the **end** of your **"self,"** the path **forward** will become **clear...**

There will come times over the course of your life together that will be hard to walk through for one or both of you. In those times, we must lean into our relationship with Christ, but we must lean into our partner for support as well. The burden of such trials most often hits one of you head-on, and your partner can feel helpless in what they can do about it.

God begins where *you* end. At the end of your "self," the path forward will become clear to those of you willing to hand that burden over to Him. What we have learned is that God placed our partner right there beside us to be His hands and His feet to help carry some of that "weight" our trials may bear. It is when one of you can walk no farther in the heaviest of trials, that the other may need to "pick up" their partner and help take that next step for you both.

SEEK SYMMETRY, NOT SUBMISSION

When merging the journeys of two travelers, there will be different approaches, styles, and habits each of you have built a life around in your individual journeys so far. It is likely that many of the things that attract you to your partner are due to the things you both have in common. The thing is that the closer the two of you walk together on this Emmaus Road to Marriage, the more likely you are to discover the differences you both have as well.

In our journey, we've discovered that there are four main areas in which the two of us needed to "get on the same page." We prefer to look at this as intentionally seeking symmetry through honesty, compromise, and respect. Those areas being: finances/budgeting, "single" parenting, child discipline, and health habits. All of these areas intertwine in some way, but each area also bears their own unique challenges.

Now, God didn't bring the two of you together so that one of you would lord over the other. Marriage was not designed by God to be a dictatorship, but God also didn't design marriage to be a democracy either. It is essential for there to be leaders and followers.

You both possess unique gifts, talents, and experiences that can work to bless your marriage, but that does not make either of you "better" than your partner. Leadership of the different areas of your blended journey cannot be controlled by or fall upon just one of you.

The leadership of your marriage must be flexible, it must be shared, and the truth is that you both can't lead the same thing at the same time either. Someone must lead, and the other must follow. Now, don't take this wrong and tell your partner to get behind you and do what I say. That is not how leadership, especially servant leadership, works. The leader and the follower should still be walking side by side in the task at hand, but that leadership can be handed back and forth as needed.

Budgeting: We are not here to tell you what your budget should be or how much you should budget for expenses you may share. For some couples, their financial blessings or baggage they bring to the relationship may have a significant impact that should not come as a surprise *after* the "I do."

Points like renting/buying a home, current debt, spending habits, and normal income need to have open and ongoing dialogue within a couple. To not do so prior to marriage can cover up some pretty big land mines you may step on later in your marriage. Again, we are not telling you what your household finances need to look like, but a foundational factor of a biblical marriage is an open set of books to balance.

"Single" parenting is a phrase we assume all of you have heard before, but our view likely takes a different approach. When we talk about "single parenting," we are not talking about divorced parents of children. For us, "single parenting" is the concept where both parents (or both sets of parents) need to be "one" in the overall approach to how your children will be parented. Now, this does not mean that everyone sits down in a room until all the rules are agreed to by everyone. That is not likely or practical, but in our experience the parents of children must be on the same team when seeking a biblical marriage.

> Take the **_time_** to put together an **_honest inventory of your_** parenting "_rules_"...

Things like curfews, cell phone use, spank or no spank, rules of the house, and the many areas in which parents influence their children need as much clarity for all the parents involved. Take the time to put together an honest inventory of your parenting "rules" each of you bring to the mix so that operating as a "single" parent becomes a blessing and not continual points of conflict.

Child discipline is another subject that falls under the "single parenting" scope in many ways, but it is a point that benefits from further clarification. The point we wish to make is that children need rules that are supported through relationships. We have heard on several occasions that children need rules and consistency in the enforcement of those rules.

If your "rule" is backed up with the words "because I said so," you are not building a trusting relationship with that child. If you cannot offer a sincere "why," then that "rule" may need a second look. In general, as a child grows up through the years of their life, their "rules" must grow as well. The "rules" children learn in childhood are what grow into lifelong Christian values through trusted relationships with their parents.

The Bible in many ways is a set of "rules" established by God (our "single" parent). He will blend His values into our lives as our relationship with Him grows. We also believe that Christ didn't sacrifice His life for our sins to only preach the "rules" we must live by.

Ultimately, we believe that a Christian life, and moreover a Christian marriage, needs the discipline of the Bible's "rules." That "discipline" as children of God is what grows into a meaningful relationship with Jesus as we live out Christ's values.

Another area in a marriage that is greatly benefited by symmetry is your health habits. Let's face it. The health habits for many of us today are just not what they could be or should be. When talking about you and your partner's health habits, we are including the body, mind, and spirit aspects of being healthy in that equation.

The spirit and mind aspects of your marriage health are most impacted through the prayer, study, and action that is incorporated into your faith journey together. That is addressed further in other sessions of this program, but the health of a Christian marriage is equally as affected by the bodily health habits you and your partner share as well.

We are not diet "gurus" here to preach the latest fad diet programs, but we have seen the direct benefits of having good health habits that align with each other. Take the time to evaluate where you and your partner can better align your bodily health. Effective yet realistic things like portion control, sharing of meals, regular exercise, and smart snacking are just a few habits that have worked wonders for us as we engaged in the symmetry of our good health habits.

Raising Your Voice

Our house is a trilevel that is not as "open concept" as we would like it to be. We jokingly have one of those "analog" paging systems in our house that we use quite often. By "analog" we mean shouting from one floor to the other. Yelling from floor to floor may work sometimes, but yelling at your partner is simply not acceptable in God's eyes. While "analog paging" may not be the best form of communication for a couple, raising your voice in anger to your partner or in an attempt to control them is an absolute sign of disrespect, and it will eat away at the very foundation of any marriage that contains such actions.

Raising one's voice in anger at your partner is not a means in which to "win" an argument, and it never should be. If "shouting down" your partner to affect the outcome you want is forcing their silence, then we would contend that your "why" was likely weak and selfish.

We ask you to commit to each other that this type of "communication" must not be used, and if it is mistakenly put into play, then agree to stop and resume with the respect that is needed. You may even need to reapproach with the humility of a sincere apology and tempered emotions.

What Are Your Strengths & Weaknesses?

> We **all** have our *strengths* and weaknesses that **we** bring to the *relationship* table.

What are you good at? What is your partner good at? What are you not good at? Do your strengths complement each other, or do your weaknesses compound with each other? We all have our strengths and weaknesses that we bring to the relationship table. Oftentimes we may not have evaluated how our strengths or weaknesses may best blend to bless our marriage.

This goes back to leadership in the relationship as well. The person with the greatest strength in managing finances may best serve the marriage by leading in this area. To make that distinction, a couple needs to take a deeper look into who they truly are.

In the evolution of your relationship, you both likely have picked up on some of the more obvious strengths or weaknesses you both have. Start with the clearest strengths or weaknesses you can agree on and work toward addressing the impact of those first. Through a process of identification and evaluation, you both will be wasting less relationship resources and creating better opportunities for your marriage's success.

I Got You

When we say, "I got you," we are pointing out that your partner needs to know that you will be there for them when things get hard. It may be an emotional need to just be present in a trying situation, or it may be as simple as the physical need of your help finishing a task they could not. The central "need" here is that your partner needs to trust that when you see something harmful to their well-being, that you will take action on their behalf. We simply cannot do it all. Your partner may see issues or concerns that you may not, and it is their responsibility to have your back.

There have been times when one of us has fallen short on a commitment, and we needed the other to step in and help. This is a certain level of sacrifice whereby you are placing your needs aside and placing the needs of your partner's struggle above your own. You need to be cautious that you are not enabling your partner's willful disregard of a danger or risk either. Every choice we make (or do not make) has consequences with some good, and some not so good. Be cautious. Picking up the slack of a reckless or lazy partner day in and day out is not a sacrifice. It is you being a doormat to their irresponsibility, and that is not having each other's back at all. Don't be a doormat.

When someone makes fun of or puts down your partner, what do you do? Do you laugh along with it and add your own jabs, or do you push back in the conversation in defense of your partner? The point of "having each other's back" is not following your partner blindly without thinking either. Most of the time, it may simply mean to "show up" and support the other in situations that may cause them pain, hurt, or embarrassment. It also means to be there to share in the work that needs to be done and the joy to be experienced. It is important to realize that your partner genuinely feels you are for them and not against them.

People With Problems

Their problems are your problems, but they are the owner. Be cautious here because you cannot be the one to fix your partner's problem alone. Ownership is key here. Engaging the issue *with* your partner is what we are asking you to do. Offering your presence, a listening ear, or even your advice is acceptable. Notice the word is *offer* and not *force*. When you are the one facing the problem, be open to asking for the support or advice from your partner as well. Many times, when a new perspective is added to a problem, the solution is more easily found.

Sacrifice: The Gift of You

Just as Christ gave himself for us, each of you will have opportunities to make sacrifices for the other. That is a genuine part of living out your Christian faith in the relationship you both have. As we stated before, you cannot allow ongoing sacrifice to turn into either of you being a doormat, but sacrifice along with compromise are intimately necessary in a successful marriage. Be that gift that keeps on giving.

Sacrifice comes in all shapes, sizes, and forms. Sacrifice is simply support but with a personal cost for yourself. That cost will vary wildly. Many sacrifices will fall well short of what Christ did for each of us. The key attribute of a genuine sacrifice is love. The giving of yourself for your partner's benefit is an act of love that shines Christ's light in your marriage. So, lean in, love out loud, and share the gift of *you*!

LEAD LIKE THE LORD OF LOVE

> ... **Christ** leads by *example* and **shows us** that the way to **lead** is through *love*.

Leadership comes in many forms, but marriage leadership is *not* lordship. Many times, in many ways, we have begun a prayer to Jesus with the words "Lord and Heavenly Father..." when facing a trial or need. Now, we are not disputing that title for Him. Christ lives through many names, and for us, Jesus is also lord of our lives.

The key takeaway here is that even though Christ has all power and authority and could easily force us to do His bidding, he does not "lord" over us and force us to do anything. Rather, Christ leads by example and shows us that the way to lead is through love.

Christ does not *demand* we follow Him. He *asks* us to follow Him. This is Christ leading us through His humble example of servant leadership. The beautiful thing is that both of you can be servant leaders within your own relationship and marriage. A Christ-centered marriage does not use force to compel action. A Christ-centered marriage uses love to lead the way. We encourage you both to seek a Christ-centered marriage where you will lead and not lord—with love.

FOR THE ROAD - LEADERSHIP & SUPPORT

As you consider these questions, please reference *Your Emmaus Roadmap to Marriage* so that you can capture your progress and any thoughts you may need to revisit from this session.

1. What are some ways in which you could utilize servant leadership to strengthen your relationship?

2. Do either of you see areas where improved support would be beneficial to your relationship? If so, what does that look like?

SESSION 6

Pursuit & Intimacy

Preparing the Way – Impact Verses

Over the next week, read the following passages. We recommend reading them at the beginning of each day so that they are kept at the top of your mind. This will help you to think and meditate on them more easily as you go about your day. Pray over them and ask God to reveal His insights on each verse.

Colossians 3:19 (NIV) "Husbands, love your wives and do not be harsh with them."

Deuteronomy 6:5 (ESV) "You shall love the LORD your God with all your heart and with all your soul and with all your might."

Matthew 22:37-38 (ESV) "And he said to him, "You shall love the Lord your God with all your heart and with all your soul and with all your mind. This is the great and first commandment."

Genesis 2:24-25 (ESV) "Therefore, a man shall leave his father and his mother and shall become united and cleave to his wife, and they shall become one flesh. And the man and his wife were both naked and were not embarrassed or ashamed in each other's presence."

Walking with Him – Teaching Points

Now that you've spent time in prayerful reflection on the Impact Verses, consider the following teaching points we have based on these verses.

It's a Date

Date nights, be they routine or surprise, are effective means in which either of you can strengthen your intimate connections and show your partner that you still pursue them. The demands of your lives may benefit from scheduling a date night or two each month to keep from pushing this special time off your plates. Planning is perfectly okay, but keep in mind that even a scheduled date needs a little spice sprinkled into the elements of pursuing your partner.

Date nights need not be at night either. Dating can honestly be any time of the day or week. Don't just relegate this special time together to the typical Friday- or Saturday-night suppers. A date night is meant to say to your partner that you value your time with them. To genuinely call that time together a date night, you should be able to pick out the elements of pursuit. Without that pursuit of your partner's heart, then your time together would be better labeled a "managers meeting."

Yes, discussing the nuts and bolts of your family is completely fine while on these dates, but your partner needs to feel that this time is just about the two of you as well. Date nights can be an effective fuel for the flames of passion and pursuit in your marriage. Ask yourself this: If you are not pursuing their heart as a priority in your relationship, then what are you pursuing?

Make the Time to Take the Time

Yes, date nights are a form of making time for each other, but the deeper part of this point is that the pursuit of your partner is like the care given to growing a rose bush in the garden. Like a rose, a marital relationship needs small yet consistent weeding and watering. Grand gestures of dedication and passion are great, but it is truly the culmination of the "little things," those intentional moments of showing your partner that they mean something, that enrich your relationship the best.

How "I Love You" Matters

There are a thousand and one ways to say "I love you" to your partner. Your partner truly needs to hear "I love you" from you as clearly and as often as possible. Like we stated before, when necessary, use words.

We, as living breathing human beings, listen with all of our senses. So, it would stand to reason that when trying to communicate "I love you" to our partner, we should seek to use as many of our senses as possible to *say*, "I love you." This goes along with the love languages that you both would have identified in the prior session when we spoke about Gary Chapman's *The 5 Love Languages*.

In essence, the two primary modes of communication are verbal and nonverbal. Verbal communication is simply the words we speak, while nonverbal communication can be a subtle combination or complex mix of the other four senses. Many times, you may not be aware of the actual nonverbal cues you are giving when saying "I love you" to your partner.

> **Date nights** can be an ***effective*** fuel for the **flames** of passion and **pursuit** in your *marriage*.

Some examples of a nonverbal "I love you" would be:

- Sight - wearing a favorite outfit they like to see you in
- Touch - gently drawing your hand across theirs while driving in the car
- Taste - preparing a special snack that they enjoy
- Smell - putting on a special cologne or perfume they gave you before you go out for dinner

Again, the ways to say "I love you" are near endless, but they all have one attribute in common. That attribute is—a choice. All expressions of love, be it a momentary glance across the table or even the sparkle of a new wedding band, require you to choose your partner. Be it your first date or your fiftieth anniversary, at your partner's core is someone who longs to be chosen, pursued, worthy, and loved. Is that not what Jesus says to each of us? Jesus says we are chosen, Jesus says we are wanted, Jesus says we are worthy, and most certainly Jesus says we are loved.

> … at your ***partner's* core** is someone who **longs** to be **chosen**, pursued, ***worthy***, and **loved**.

You, yes *you*, are an intimate means of Christ's love for your partner. God tells us He loves us through His word in the Bible. His son, Christ Jesus, showcased that love in His time here on earth. Mary of Bethany smelled love in the perfume she poured on Jesus's feet. The leper could feel the love when Jesus healed him with His touch. The disciples tasted love in that last meal they shared with Jesus, and it was the world who saw love when Christ hung on that cross. I love you–*taste* it, *smell* it, *feel* it, *see* it, or *say* it. The how? Well, that choice is up to you!

X's & O's

We hope the game tic-tac-toe is not the first thing you think of when you think of X's & O's. The X's & O's we are actually talking about are the hugs and kisses the two of you share.

Embracing your partner is so much more connective than the simplicity of a hug may imply. The same goes for kissing as well. While things can get steamy at times (we hope so), kissing your partner is a simple yet vastly complex form of creating connection with them. The *quantity* of the hugs and kisses the two of you share is an important factor, but it is the *quality* and duration of those moments that will bear the most fruit in your marriage.

The critical point here is that quality is so much more important than quantity when it comes to your kisses and hugs. Consider thinking about it this way. You are not "getting" a kiss or hug from your partner in all of this. You need to approach these opportunities as a time to "give" your partner the quality of connection and depth of peace you both need for journey together with Christ. All of this can lead the two of you on a much more positive path to greater intimacy and connection in the life you share.

TO PURSUE TAKES TWO

> **Deep** down, we *all* want to be **wanted**.

This version of pursuit is not trivial (pun intended) by any means. The pursuit of your partner's heart and soul will require *your* heart and soul to do so. In some form or another, we all want to be wanted. Just as the police may use all types of means or methods to apprehend their suspect, you should also use varied ways in which to pursue your partner.

The path you use or the path they use for the "hunt" will likely not look the same. Things like texting, phone calls, emails, physical touch, a hidden note, and even a card in the mail are just a few of the many ways in which you can genuinely pursue your partner. Be creative, be spontaneous, but most importantly be *you*. We have taken bits and pieces of other couples' experiences to help us continually evolve our pursuit of each other, and so should you. Some routines are good, but be careful not to make your pursuit a check-the-box type of to-do list either.

Deep down, we all want to be wanted. Playing a little "hard to get" can add some fun to the mix, but you can't pursue your partner if you are not moving toward them in some way. Christ continually pursues each of us out of His love and desire to be His, and His alone. Shouldn't we do the same for the one we seek to share our soul?

SOCIAL-ME-TAH-YUH, *NOT* SOCIAL-MEE-DEE-YUH

You can't pursue your partner with your phone in front of your face. The world is filled with enough attention-seekers needing one more "like" on their perfect post, so the internet won't collapse without your review and reply.

Social-me-tah-yuh represents our blending of the phrase "social me to you." When we say, "social me to you," we are pointing to that personal one-to-one connection with your partner that is necessary for a successful marriage. You may have guessed that "social-mee-dee-yuh" is talking about that wide internet world of "social me-d-ia."

The point here is to *put down your phone*, spend time with your partner, and not with those various social media platforms you may be a part of. This leads to our universal point that a key need we believe every person has is "to be seen." It stands to reason that where your eyes are *is* your priority.

To meet the need that your partner has to be seen, we as a society need to carve time away from the screens we seem to worship so easily. Now, this does not mean all social media is a waste of time. It has the ability to connect us with people and events not so near to us, but it cannot displace the precious time we need to see the people right in front of us.

We have found that social media is very helpful in sharing moments of our lives with the extended family and friends we have. We have also found that our overuse of social media was pulling us away from our intimate connection as well.

As Christians, we need to lift our eyes to Jesus, and as a Christian couple, we also need to lift our eyes to each other. Making a beautiful post about your partner's birthday or sharing a funny video of dogs who talk is completely fine as a small part of you and your partner's connection profile. The key to that statement is "small part."

We have long held the belief that *anything* to excess can become *sin* in your life. It may be your phone, it may be your job, it may be a hobby, but whatever "*it*" is could be that "*thing*" in your life that is making your partner feel they are not worthy of being seen. So, what is it that you choose to see?

FOR THE ROAD - PURSUIT & INTIMACY

As you consider these questions, please reference *Your Emmaus Roadmap to Marriage* so that you can capture your progress and any thoughts you may need to revisit from this session.

1. What are some creative ways in which you could say "I love you"?
2. Is there a need in your relationship to change your social media use habits? If so, what would that look like?
3. How do you feel that you meet that need of your partner to feel wanted and desired? What are some possibilities to improve that?

SESSION 7

PRIVACY & PROTECTION

PREPARING THE WAY – IMPACT VERSES

Over the next week, read the following passages. We recommend reading them at the beginning of each day so that they are kept at the top of your mind. This will help you to think and meditate on them more easily as you go about your day. Pray over them and ask God to reveal His insights on each verse.

Ecclesiastes 4:12 (NIV) "Though one may be overpowered, two can defend themselves. A cord of three strands is not quickly broken."

1 Corinthians 13:4-7 (NIV) "Love is patient, love is kind. It does not envy, it does not boast, it is not proud. It does not dishonor others, it is not self-seeking, it is not easily angered, it keeps no record of wrongs. Love does not delight in evil but rejoices with the truth. It always protects, always trusts, always hopes, always perseveres."

2 Thessalonians 3:3 (ESV) "But the Lord is faithful. He will establish you and guard you against the evil one."

Ephesians 6:11 (NIV) "Put on the full armor of God, so that you can take your stand against the devil's schemes." (We suggest verses 12-17 as well.)

Psalms 91:2 (NIV) "I will say of the Lord, "He is my refuge and my fortress, my God, in whom I trust."

Proverbs 9:10-11 (NIV) "The fear of the Lord is the beginning of wisdom, and knowledge of the Holy One is understanding. For through wisdom your days will be many, and years will be added to your life."

Walking with Him – Teaching Points

Now that you've spent time in prayerful reflection on the Impact Verses, consider the following teaching points we have based on these verses.

Keep Your Dirt in Your Own Backyard

We have found in recent years that more and more couples have resorted to "public trials" on social media in order to win what should have been a private marital dispute. We are not talking about resolving where to eat dinner on a Friday night and things like that. What we are pointing out is that when you enlist others in a public format to "build your case" or justify your position in an argument, your lack of privacy is undermining the trust in your marriage.

Reaching out to mutually trusted accountability couples or friends who are a part of your inner circle of trust is not a form of trial by public opinion. When a disagreement on a more private subject cannot be resolved, then we wholeheartedly recommend seeking out those types of mutually trusted people in your life. A different perspective or added bit of wisdom may provide you with greater understanding for a better solution or compromise. The privacy of your conflict is a factor that can directly impact the trust the two of you share. This goes back to the point of not trying to "win" the arguments you may have, but rather seeking a solution based on wisdom and what you truly need.

Rise Up When They Cannot

Let's face it, the two of you have or absolutely will face some sort of deep hurt or loss that may literally bring one of you to your knees. It is in those times that you must rise up to protect and love your partner as God has asked you to. This may look like you taking both cell phones and filtering the difficult calls that may come, or it may be you taking lead for a while in areas of your marriage that are typically theirs. Regardless of the task, some situations you may face during your marriage will require one of you to rise up when the other cannot.

This also goes for those most joyous of times you may share in the course of your marriage. It may be the birth of a child or even the starting of a new job, but even these times may need the other to rise up in that season of excitement.

Trust *IN* Your Privacy

Trust is a critical component to the privacy a marriage needs for you both to feel safe and secure. Let's face it, there will be events, sensitive information, or plans your partner may have that need your full discretion and confidential treatment. In most relationships, this is simply called keeping a secret. You should not keep secrets *from* your partner, but it is perfectly fine to keep secrets *with* your partner.

Personal information or situations that are shared between the two of you need to have clear rules of engagement when it comes to who else may be told or what details may be divulged. This way harmful errors in communication do not occur, and the trust shared between the two of you is maintained.

The Battle is Real: Know Where to Stand

So, where is it that you stand with your partner? The physical and spiritual enemies in this world will seek to tear down, deceive, and destroy a marriage that is centered on Christ. It does not matter if you are six foot four or four foot six, the "warrior spirit" God placed within you must be willing and ready to protect your partner, so put on your Armor of God and stand up to the sin of this world *with* your partner.

> **...so** put on your **Armor** of **God** and **stand up** to the sin of this **world WITH** your *partner*.

Some dangers to a Christian marriage will come at one or both of you head-on regardless of your physical strength or spiritual depth. There will come a time when one of you will need to stand up to that evil when the other is not able to. Be it a past addiction, slanderous gossip, or "devil at your door," your marriage will need you to stand at the front of the battle the two of you are facing. Have faith in your armor (God fit it especially to you), but also remember you are never ever alone in these battles you shall face.

There are some dangers your marriage will face that will require the two of you to stand side by side when facing the enemy before you. Battles like the threat of false accusations or the results of a biopsy are such times in which your marriage will need the strength of you *both* to weather the waves crashing against you. This is where understanding your strengths and weaknesses becomes most critical. Your blend of gifts, talents, and wisdom are also your weapons in defeating the foes your marriage will face.

There is yet one final place you may need to stand in the "world's war" facing your marriage, and that is back-to-back. This is when it seems like the enemy has surrounded you and the battle may be all but lost. We pray your marriage never faces such a battlefield, but it is here where the depth of your resolve and the foundation of your marriage will be revealed. God does not provide His armor so that we may polish it to shine in the sun. He gave His armor to us so that we may go to battle with His son at our side as well.

The battle up to this point is likely to have come with personal losses that have been written into lasting scars. Our prayer is that you have persevered and are able to claim victory in Christ's name. The neat thing is that though your scars may be a chapter written by war with the world, they are only a small part of the story Christ will write as you walk your "Emmaus Road to Marriage" with Him.

Guard the Gate *WITH* Jesus

We have spoken about standing with our partner in the battles our marriage may face, but we must also be vigilant in times of peace as well. We liken our marriage to a fortress God has given the two of us. Jesus may stand at the gate of our marriage and yours, but He does not say that He alone will guard the gate. We must stand *with* Jesus at the gate to keep watch against the evil that may seek to enter our fortress and defeat us from within.

In times of peace, we cannot let down our guard. Standing guard is made most effective by enhancing our awareness with wisdom. All too often, we spiral down the rabbit hole of worry when we do not allow wisdom to be a key part of guarding the gate. The main point here is that awareness that lacks wisdom is just worry, and worry will work to undermine your marriage as well.

Fear: Awareness without Wisdom

Part of protecting yourself and your partner is simply being more aware of the world around you. For us, awareness is essential for a life filled with greater peace and less worry. Be cautious not to let awareness become worrying by allowing unrealistic fear or a lack of information define your present circumstances.

SESSION 7: Privacy & Protection

Both of you have a distinct set of life experiences that support the wisdom either of you apply to what you are collectively exposed to each day. There is a terrific book we have read that provides realistic insight into how to use the fear we may experience as wisdom for our awareness. We highly recommend you read and discuss between the two of you a book named *The Gift of Fear*, by Gavin de Becker (1999). For us, this book helped us to see how understanding fear can provide wisdom and strength.

> *...understanding* **Fear** can **provide** *wisdom* and **strength.**

Fear is a natural feeling that is okay to have regardless of how tough or "trained" you may feel you are. When you combine the fear you may feel with information and understanding, then you create awareness that helps to protect you and your partner. Fear is a useful tool in the devil's arsenal of deception. Fear without proper understanding will work to undermine every area of your marriage. Fear will control your marriage if left unchecked by the wisdom God has provided you.

FOR THE ROAD - PRIVACY & PROTECTION

As you consider these questions, please reference *Your Emmaus Roadmap to Marriage* so that you can capture your progress and any thoughts you may need to revisit from this session.

1. Has your relationship faced "battles" in which you needed to stand with your partner? If not, how could you be better prepared to do so?

2. How can fear play a positive role in your relationship? Are there times in your lives that can be used to turn fear into wisdom?

SESSION 8

MODELING & PRAISE

PREPARING THE WAY – IMPACT VERSES

Over the next week, read the following passages. We recommend reading them at the beginning of each day so that they are kept at the top of your mind. This will help you to think and meditate on them more easily as you go about your day. Pray over them and ask God to reveal His insights on each verse.

Ephesians 4:29 (NIV) "Do not let any unwholesome talk come out of your mouths, but only what is helpful for building others up according to their needs, that it may benefit those who listen."

Song of Songs 4:7 (NIV) "You are altogether beautiful, my darling; there is no flaw in you."

Hebrews 6:10-12 (New King James Version) "For God *is* not unjust to forget your work and labor of love which you have shown toward His name, *in that* you have ministered to the saints, and do minister. And we desire that each one of you show the same diligence to the full assurance of hope until the end, that you do not become sluggish, but imitate those who through faith and patience inherit the promises."

1 Thessalonians 5:11 (NIV) "Therefore encourage one another and build each other up, just as in fact you are doing."

Isaiah 64:8 (NIV) "Yet you, Lord, are our Father. We are the clay, you are the potter; we are all the work of your hand."

WALKING WITH HIM – TEACHING POINTS

Now that you've spent time in prayerful reflection on the Impact Verses, consider the following teaching points we have based on these verses.

THE POWER OF PRAISE

That first line of the doxology, "Praise God from whom all blessings flow" declares such a beautiful truth of what praise means to God. If praise is so important to God, shouldn't we model His character and seek to praise our partner as well with no less of our heart?

> The **key** to **praise** is that *it must* be grounded with *truth* and rooted in reality.

It has been our overwhelming experience that the power of praise can have significant and lasting effects on the positive growth in most any relationship, but especially in a Christ-centered marriage. Genuine and sincere praise creates positive connections between the desirable actions and the blessings we can share with our partner.

The key to praise is that it must be grounded with truth and rooted in reality. Hollow praise that is not based on actual accomplishments and facts will actually work to undermine established trust that you have. Adding additional aspects like positivity and hope to the scope of your partner's praise helps to strengthen their spirit, which in turn makes your marriage fertile ground for continued growth.

Painting a picture of "puppy dogs and rainbows" by overpraising your partner will eat away at your relationship and may even lead to making your partner prideful. The

> There is **power** in your **praise**, so **use** it *wisely*.

problem with empty praise is that the receiver can end up blindly unaware of the reality in which they live. Given enough time, it may be too late to correct your course to avoid future pain and heartache.

In those moments when one of you may fail, praise needs to be tempered with accountability and grace. We all fall short of our potential. That is just a cold hard fact. We all have likely fallen prey to the deception of false praise as well. It is a solid connection between the two of you and Christ that will help both of you provide and receive praise in ways that bless you both.

The critical point here is that praise *must* be genuine. Praise is a powerful tool in building Christ's kingdom, yet false praise is as powerful a tool as well with which the devil can easily sow his seeds of lies and deception. There is power in your praise, so use it wisely.

To Model and Mold

Whether your life's journey together will have, already has, or won't have children as a part of your family, it is exceedingly important you model the man or woman you desire for others to seek for their journey. The fact is that each day after our daughters first opened their eyes to us, we have been the models of what a husband and wife are in this world. Early on in our marriage, we were not consistent in our modeling of a Christ-centered couple to our two girls. We felt we were good enough, but the farther we walked on our Emmaus Road with Christ, we realized that good enough is not enough.

What we began to see was that the husband and wife we were to each other were the models our girls were using as a template for their future relationships. The problem was that we didn't necessarily model a Christ-centered marriage as well as we thought we were. Now, don't get us wrong, we did a lot of good things too, but we knew we could be better for our girls. It was that realization that fueled our passion to put this program together.

Here are some questions you may want to consider:

- As a husband, would I have peace in knowing my son was looking to marry a woman that would love and honor him like I have been loved and honored by his mother?

- As a wife, would I have peace in knowing my son would love and honor his wife as I have been loved and honored by his father?

- As a husband, would I have peace knowing my daughter was loving and honoring her husband just as I was loving and honoring her mother?

- As a wife, would I have peace in knowing my daughter was loving and honoring her husband just as I was loving and honoring her father?

If you do not find peace in one or more of these questions that focus on you, then it is time for you to make some very important decisions about who you are for your children. Remember, to do nothing is still a decision you have made.

We believe this Emmaus Road to marriage we are asking you to walk is a realistic means in which the two of you can find greater peace for your Christ-centered marriage. Christ asks each of us to follow Him, walk with Him, have faith like Him, live like Him, be like Him, and most importantly—love like Him. Christ is the model we can use to mold ourselves into as we choose to walk with Him each day.

Success Through Mentorship & Accountability

> Mentorship combined **with** *relationship* is what creates **effective accountability.**

You are not the first couple to face the loss of a job. You are not the first couple to navigate the numerous trials of parenting. You are not the first couple that doubted their faith either. There are other mature Christian couples that have walked similar paths to yours. Their experiences and wisdom are another means in which God can bless your marriage through mentorship.

To us, in the context of marriage, mentorship is more focused on each one of you for your growth as an individual. It is very unlikely that a mentor will just show up at your front door. You first need to acknowledge your need for growth, and then you need to go out and look for a mentor to work on your marriage with. For our purposes, a mentor is more focused on the "how to fish" discipleship of achieving your goals and does not "fish" for you.

When it comes to a successful Christ-centered marriage, we need the discipleship of other Christian couples. That "team" form of mentorship is what we call an accountability couple. Mentorship combined with relationship is what creates effective accountability. Accountability couples are mentors for each of you as individuals, but it does not stop there. It is their mentorship of your marriage while still focusing on Christ that makes the real difference on your Emmaus Road to marriage.

Genuine Christ-centered accountability with another couple should look like:

- Routine individual meetings of the "guys" or the "gals" to discuss life, goals, struggles, joys, etc... the format, means, frequency, and focus should be flexible, but have some sort of agreed to structure.

- Routine meetings of all four of you to digest some of those individual concerns or group concerns, but with the focus turned toward the growth of the marriage relationship.

- Not every time, but physically be in the same room when discussing more difficult issues. Video chats can be a very good means in which to "see" each other, but a phone call check in is better than nothing at all.

- These meetings must be a safe space for open and honest discussion of sensitive information. **Confidentiality is crucial here.**

- There should *never* be any secrets held between you and the accountability couple that exclude your partner. Now, for example, we would not view one wife telling the other wife about how a bad argument hurt her, but after a proper amount of discernment, the four of you need to work on the issue together.

- We have an understanding that everything discussed within the scope of these meetings is eventually known by each person. Using the prior example, we would strongly encourage the mentoring couple to process the concerns she heard about from the other wife with each other as well.

- Honesty, openness, transparency, confidentiality, sympathy, and empathy are all critical components to the effectiveness of mentoring and couple accountability.

One final but noteworthy point about having an accountability couple for your marriage is that the support and mentoring is truly for *both* couples. The road goes both ways. Every marriage needs to know it is not alone, and discipleship through accountability couples can do just that.

Which Wolf Will You Feed?

As we have walked our own Emmaus Road of marriage, we have also learned that our mental health and our physical health are intimately connected for our overall wellness. The health of your marriage and relationship as a couple are much the same.

> The **wisdom** of the *story* lies **in** the **grandfather's** response, "The **one** you **feed**."

There is an old Cherokee story we heard of called "The Two Wolves." In short, it tells of two wolves who are fighting that represent the good and evil within us. It is typically told from the perspective of a young man asking his grandfather about which wolf will win. The wisdom of the story lies in the grandfather's response, "The one you feed."

Every one of us has those same two wolves within us who are battling for our soul. Which wolf are you feeding within you? More importantly, which wolf are you feeding for your partner? The obvious answer we wish to give is the good wolf, but let's not deceive ourselves. The evil wolf within each of us easily feeds each day on the sin and negative thoughts we too frequently have.

That battle is an ongoing struggle that each of us must navigate as best as possible, and that same battle is one we must fight for our marriages as well. The health of your body and mind as individuals "feed" those "wolves" inside each of you. The building of positive pathways within your mind and marriage are a key means of feeding the good wolves within each of us.

A few ways to provide good and healthy foods for the spiritual battles ahead are:

- regular study/reading of God's word
- frequent prayer (privately, together, and for others)
- encouraging comments (and praise) for your partner
- the repetition of positive thoughts within yourself
- processing issues with your accountability couple
- memorizing impact verses to use in the battle
- worshiping God with your Christian community

It is also just as important to "feed" your physical body the best foods for the battle as well. A few of the physical things we can feed our bodies are:

SESSION 8: Modeling & Praise

- regular exercise with a balanced blend of high and low impact routines–do what works for *you*
- a balanced diet of actual foods that help maintain a heart-healthy weight
- a doctor advised scope of vitamins, minerals, or supplements to aid in your activity and energy
- minimize the intake of those "snack machine" foods you love to hate

In this story of "The Two Wolves," the survival of your marriage and relationship feeds off the "good" and "evil" things that each of you provide. We are in no way telling you this will be easy, but we do know that for us, our marriage is worth the hard work we put into it. We believe that when your "good wolves" stand side by side in this battle, there is the mighty Lion of Judah standing there with you who is fighting for your marriage as well. It is with Him, our lord Jesus Christ and the heavenly banquet He provides, that we are able to taste the sweetest victories in the battles that lie before us all.

FOR THE ROAD - MODELING & PRAISE

As you consider these questions, please reference *Your Emmaus Roadmap to Marriage* so that you can capture your progress and any thoughts you may need to revisit from this session.

1. What are some ways in which you could possibly use praise to build up your partner?
2. Has there been a role model or mentor in your life that impacted you? If so, what aspects of them spoke the most to your spirit?
3. Which "wolf" do you feel you are feeding? What are some ways that you could improve what you feed your body and spirit?

SESSION 9

PROJECTS & WORK

PREPARING THE WAY – IMPACT VERSES

Over the next week, read the following passages. We recommend reading them at the beginning of each day so that they are kept at the top of your mind. This will help you to think and meditate on them more easily as you go about your day. Pray over them and ask God to reveal His insights on each verse.

Genesis 2:18 (NIV) "The Lord God said, 'It is not good for the man to be alone. I will make a helper suitable for him.'"

Psalm 46:1 (ESV) "God is our refuge and strength, a very present help in trouble."

Ecclesiastes 4:9-10 (NIV) "Two are better than one, because they have a good return for their labor: If either of them falls down, one can help the other up. But pity anyone who falls and has no one to help them up."

Romans 12:4-5 (NIV) "For just as each of us has one body with many members, and these members do not all have the same function, so in Christ we, though many, form one body, and each member belongs to all the others."

WALKING WITH HIM – TEACHING POINTS

Now that you've spent time in prayerful reflection on the Impact Verses, consider the following teaching points we have based on these verses.

To-Dos & To-Dones

The best way to get something done is actually pretty basic. The main thing is that you have to start doing whatever "it" is. You may have heard it be called the "honey-do" list or simply the "to-do" list, but regardless of its name, such a list is not a bad thing to have for projects either of you need done. We are not talking about common tasks like sweeping a floor or folding a basket of clothes. The list we are speaking of is an actual list of the projects you desire to be done for the improvement or enhancement of your life together. A "to-do" list is only worth the paper it is written on unless you choose to make those items on the list a priority for your partnership.

"To-dos" won't become "to-dones" without one of you taking the lead for that project. That only makes sense when considering it is likely that the one who added it has the greatest desire to get it done. We are not telling you this to overcomplicate things. We believe this is a key point for a successful marriage because for us, no plan usually means no progress.

Helping each other with these special projects not only completes a needed task, but they can also be relationship building as well. Now, keep in mind the fact that difficulties may arise, and tempers may flare at times, so a little patience and a bit of grace may need to be added to the list as well.

Service: A Package Deal

> ... **for us,** no _**plan**_ **usually means** no _**progress**_.

Serving others in the name of Christ is a pillar of the Christian community. Where and how you serve are important, and we believe serving together is yet another way to strengthen your marriage and relationship even more. We are not saying you should not serve as individuals, but we are saying that there are beautiful and unique blessings that are found in that shared time of serving others side by side.

As a couple, we have served various types of ministries for our church family, and it was through those experiences that we found our passion to serve the two of you with this program in the foundational years of your marriage. Sharing in the joy of a personal victory or even sharing the weight of a bag of mulch will work to bring the two of you even closer while serving God's kingdom as His hands and feet.

Adventure Projects

Okay, so this aspect of working together has blessed us with some of the most rewarding and meaningful times of our marriage. The only thing we would have done differently was to start these adventures earlier on in our marriage. That is why we bring this to you now, so that your marriage can benefit from those lessons we have learned. You see, adventure projects are just that: adventures into the unknown that can take you a little (or a lot) out of your comfort zones. What qualifies as an adventure is truly up to you, but it needs to push the both of you to engage life in new and exciting ways.

One such adventure project was born from our shared love of an oh-so-gooey-chewy caramel as a sweet treat every now and then. That was getting a little expensive at the candy stores, so this became an opportunity for us to venture into the unexplored area of making our own caramel squares. A few internet searches and gathering the right ingredients became a simple yet beautiful way we now connect as a couple. We had a great time doing it even with the hours of stirring that were needed, but we cannot lie, we have made some really *really* good batches of caramel.

Another adventure project we undertook was the remodeling of our primary bedroom. This was no simple coat of paint and new outlet covers. We did not do all of the work alone, but for several months, we worked side by side as we tore down walls, replaced carpet, ran wire, patched holes, and of course, painted what seemed like every square inch of that room (twice . . . lol). We have worked on many projects over the years, but nothing as big as this one.

You see, we had been blindsided a few months before that by some very scary migraines for Audra. While combating these episodes and the many doctors' visits, we found that we needed to create room for a rocking chair near our bed for her to recover in. Her greatest healing came as she let the medicines work as she gently rocked in her chair, but the problem was that her rocking chair was all the way downstairs. We spent many nights in the living room and not in our bed. Leaving her alone was just not an option for us, so from that need was born this adventure project to make room for a rocking recliner beside our bed. Her "sanctuary," as we call it, has helped us heal in many ways since taking on

> *You* may just *surprise* yourself **with** how **bold** you *both* can be.

that adventure together. It was the deeper connection and appreciation for each other we created during that time that we cherish so much.

Your adventures need you to look beyond the edge of who you are right now, but not beyond your budget. Economical ways to push yourselves yet not break the bank are possible on any budget. Get creative, be adventurous, and see what lies beyond the current horizon the two of you share. You may just surprise yourself with how bold you both can be.

Give Time vs Take Time (Choice vs Obligation)

This point closely follows the need for making your partner a priority in your life, like we discussed in session one. The key here is making the conscious choice to choose your partner to do these things with. Others can be involved when needed, but keep in mind these projects are intended to help you lean into each other and not away toward others.

Doing something out of guilt or fear is not the way this works either. Open and honest communication is what will help prevent misunderstandings that will undermine genuine adventures. What also helps is maintaining the perspective that it is better to give of your time than it is to expect your partner to give you their time. Giving your partner the choice and time they desire for an adventure is not to create obligation or marriage debt with your partner. Take a sincere look at your "why" to see if you are truly *giving* or *taking* your next adventure the two of you take.

Work to Live, not Live to Work

What do you truly live for? For us, the answer has evolved over the years of our marriage. We would love to say that our jobs come second to each other, but that was not always so. You cannot dismiss the obvious need for a good-paying job to live and operate from in the life you two share.

The trouble is that we too often derive too much of our identity and worth from the job we earn a living with. It would also be naive to think a job is meaningless and bears no value to our identity as well.

We strongly believe that you both need to agree on a work-life balance that fits your situation. Be realistic but know that any gain you seek has risk and will require some form of sacrifice. Your work-life balance now will not be the same over the span of your marriage. Today's balance will likely not work five years from now. It is best to evaluate your balance at least every couple of years or when those larger events in life need the balance to change.

Your work-life balance is made up of a unique blend of family needs, benefits from your jobs, leisure activities, spiritual health, and overall health in most ways. Just as we have pointed out in much of this program, the work-life balance that meets your needs is most impacted by your shared priorities and the resources you apply to those priorities. That is where the open and honest communication you share will help you not to tip too far from each other.

Again, it all boils back to time. Time is that one commodity we all want more of but have no means to create. Our feeling is that there is no better place in which to make that time than right now. Just like you should budget your money, it is even more important to budget your time. With more time you can always earn more money, but with more money you cannot always earn more time. We suggest you "spend" your time wisely.

It may be the next five minutes you "spend" with someone you love that becomes so precious to you. None of us are guaranteed tomorrow. What is it that each of you are working to live for? With our heart of hearts, we ask you to take as many of those "five minutes" you may need each day and "invest" them wisely into the ones you love.

FOR THE ROAD - PROJECTS & WORK

As you consider these questions, please reference *Your Emmaus Roadmap to Marriage* so that you can capture your progress and any thoughts you may need to revisit from this session.

1. What may be some "adventure projects" that the two of you would like to try?
2. Does your work-life balance support your relationship success? What are some improvements that you feel would help balance things out?

SESSION 10

Now & Then

Preparing the Way – Impact Verses

Over the next week, read the following passages. We recommend reading them at the beginning of each day so that they are kept at the top of your mind. This will help you to think and meditate on them more easily as you go about your day. Pray over them and ask God to reveal His insights on each verse.

2 Peter 1:5-7 (NIV) "For this very reason, make every effort to add to your faith goodness; and to goodness, knowledge; and to knowledge, self-control; and to self-control, perseverance; and to perseverance, godliness; and to godliness, mutual affection; and to mutual affection, love."

Romans 12:2 (NKJV) "And do not be conformed to this world, but be transformed by the renewing of your mind, that you may prove what *is* that good and acceptable and perfect will of God."

Proverbs 19:20 (ESV) "Listen to advice and accept instruction, that you may gain wisdom in the future."

Jeremiah 29:11 (NIV) "For I know the plans I have for you," declares the LORD, "plans to prosper you and not to harm you, plans to give you hope and a future."

Walking with Him – Teaching Points

Now that you've spent time in prayerful reflection on the Impact Verses, consider the following teaching points we have based on these verses.

Two Tense will make you Too Tense

Who you were, who you are, and who you will become are all heavily influenced by the perspective in which you view them. When we say, "don't be two tense," we are intentionally saying the number *two* and not the T - O - O form of too. Why? Because our experience tells us that for a marriage to walk with Christ, difficulties will arise. Tension is created when either one or both of you try to live in the past "tense," the present "tense," or even in the future "tense." That is why we believe that trying to live in "two" tense will make you "too" tense.

> Trying to **live** in "**two**" *tense* will make you "***too***" **tense**.

Live right now! The present is the only time you can control. You cannot change what you may have done or what may have happened to you, but you can change the perspective in which you view those events of your past. Things like counseling, accountability groups, studying God's word, and prayer are just a few of the ways in which both of you can gain Christ-inspired wisdom to apply to the perspective in which you view your past.

The journeys each of you have traveled to get to this point have shaped much of who you are for each other. That includes all the traumas, hurts, pain, and suffering you have experienced, but that also includes all of the joys, love, praise, and victories as well. Too often we allow our past to define who we are, when what we have found is that only today defines who you really are.

You cannot live in the "past" tense and also live in the "present" tense. It is just not possible to do both. Trying to do so may seem to work for a while, but what really is happening is that the decisions you make today are the only ones that really matter. You can only give one of those "tenses" control of your spirit. Now, please understand, we are not saying that your past hasn't *influenced* who you are now, but your past does not *define* who you are today. That definition is truly up to you both as individuals, and the same goes for your marriage as well.

Be aware that you may be giving the future "tense" too much power over today as well. This power usually manifests as worry or doubt. The beautiful thing is that you can take that control back by creating realistic short- and long-term goals that will provide direction for your future together.

There may be two of you, but each of you cannot live in different "tenses." Left unchecked, letting the past or even the future hold power over today will rob your marriage of so many blessings God has for you in His plan. As you discover areas of your life you have given power over your present, work with your partner and those you trust to take that power back.

THE GOAL OF GOALS

We believe Ben Franklin said it best, "If you fail to plan, you plan to fail." The act of setting goals for more immediate or long-term needs helps the two of you to better evaluate the twists and turns life will throw at you. Maybe you have a goal of saving up to buy a more reliable car or maybe something more immediate like what to make for supper. Either way, big or small, a plan for the success of your marriage is simply an agreed to series of goals.

The goal of goals in your marriage is to provide a plan or direction that will maximize the efficiency and use of your combined resources for your ongoing success.

> "**If You** *fail* to plan, *you* **plan** to *fail*."
> —Ben Franklin

The setting of goals needs open and honest communication between the two of you to truly be effective. One of the best ways to ensure accountability and clarity of your goals is to write them down. It does not matter if they are in a note on your phone, a calendar on your wall, or even a binder with tabs, we have seen firsthand that writing down your goals can create a practical plan for your success.

Be flexible with your goals, but not too flexible. As life throws those curveballs and changeups at you, some parts of the plan may need to evolve. It may also benefit your overall plan to group the goals into time frames or categories that make sense for your journey. You are constantly making hourly, daily, and other short-term goals that may or may not benefit from being written down. Longer-term goals that go out maybe one month, six months, one year, five years, ten years, etc. . . . are best realized when they become a part of your written plan.

Check in regularly on the progress of your goals. It makes sense that your shorter-term goals will require little to no check in between the two of you. It is our experience that goals that may take weeks, months, or even years see greater success from regular check ins when written down. We are not here to tell you how you must check in, but we absolutely recommend that you set up some means to monitor and adjust your goals.

You should have both personal and shared goals as parts of your marriage plan as well. The marital goals that you both share are important to develop and monitor for your overall success. It is equally important for each of you to develop and monitor personal goals that focus on each of you individually.

Sharing these personal goals with your spouse (and maybe even your accountability couple) is highly recommended for your own accountability, but keep in mind that the responsibility still lies with you and not your partner when it comes to personal goals.

Goal Scope & Scale

Earlier in this session, we pointed out how categorizing your goals may help you with their development, management, and completion. Two things we have learned along the way are that the best goals in your life's plan are both realistic and have some means in which to measure them as well. When these two attributes are present for a goal, then action and direction are better understood in pursuit of success.

There are three main categories that we have generally grouped our personal and shared goals into. Those are: Snap goals, SMART goals, and God-sized goals.

> **SMART *goals*:** what we **see** as *measurable* **goals** for **growth**.

Snap goals are usually time-sensitive tasks that are a part of the living schedule we have each day. A Snap goal can take moments or hours, but they typically don't make it into our written plan. They may be on our phones, a small "reminder" note, or simply a part of our current activity.

SMART goals are what we see as measurable goals for growth. What SMART goals help to provide is a checklist of goal attributes that make the goal more effective and more likely to be accomplished. The SMART in SMART goals stands for: Specific, Measurable, Achievable, Relevant, and Time-Bound.

Let's look a bit closer at what SMART goals are made of:

- Specific: the goal needs to be specific and clearly identified so the *what* or What Actions that are needed is understood.

- Measurable: the goal needs to have some way that you understand *how* or *how much* you can determine your success or completion of the goal.

- Achievable: the goal needs to be realistic. *Can* this goal be reasonably accomplished or completed?

- Relevant: the goal needs to be clearly connected with the "big picture" and related to your needs. Knowing your *why* adds your passion to the goal.

- Time-Bound: the goal needs some scope of time to establish *when* it needs to be done by or when actions need to occur.

There are many great resources online that can help you to wade a bit deeper into the SMART goals pool. We encourage you both to seek out a format that fits your style of learning to better explore the use of SMART goals for you and your partner. Taking a little time here will save a lot of time later before diving into some SMART goals that fit the two of you.

God-sized goals—aka "The Bucket Listers"—these are goals that may reach beyond your current understanding or abilities, but something deep within your spirit desires this goal for yourself or your partner. A "big" difference from other goals you may have lies in how God-sized goals may actually require several SMART goals for their successful completion. God-sized goals quite often place clear stakes of accomplishment in the ground along your Emmaus Road to marriage.

One such "bucket list" type of goal we shared became a reality when we renewed our wedding vows at a small community garden in rural Indiana a few years ago. The God-sized goal we created a plan for was to write new wedding vows and renew our vows at a location where we were surrounded by natural beauty. We had to plan out several other smaller goals and milestones to make this a reality, but step by step we were able to get each of the smaller goals accomplished. With God as our witness, we were able to accomplish that God-sized goal that exciting and joyful spring day.

God-sized goals will most certainly need many smaller Snap goals and several SMART goals to create the framework of possibility for your God-sized goal to be realized.

Those "bucket list" types of goals may be personal or shared, but one aspect they likely possess is that they need you to step out in some way with faith and courage. If it bears no cost or you feel no risk, then is it truly a God-sized goal?

Let us assure you that there is no goal bigger than our God. Share your dreams with each other. A dream is really just a "God-sized" goal without a plan, so go get some paper and start planning *your* God-sized goals! Open and honest discernment can help your dreams become those "God-sized" goals that lead the two of you down a truly blessed "Emmaus Road to marriage."

For the Road - Now & Then

As you consider these questions, please reference *Your Emmaus Roadmap to Marriage* so that you can capture your progress and any thoughts you may need to revisit from this session.

1. Have you found yourselves to be "too tense" at times? What are some ways you may be able to relieve that "tense"-ion?

2. What are a few short- or longer-term goals that may benefit from putting them in the SMART goal format?

3. What would a God-sized goal look like for each of you? How can these become a reality?

OKAY
Now What?

Looking Beyond the Bend

Where do we go from here? Well, first, you both need to look back at the journey you have taken with us in this program. A Christ-centered marriage can yield some of the greatest blessings God has planned for your lives. He never said it would be easy, but Jesus did say it would be worth it when we walk with Him at our side.

Sit down (together . . . lol) and see how you have grown closer and stronger in your relationship. Go back to these sessions from time to time and refresh yourselves. Teaching points that may not have made too much sense now will likely blend right into who you are farther down the road.

Investment in marriage counseling and programs like the one you have just completed will pay off when added to your journey together. Whether it be pre-marriage, one year in, ten years in, twenty years in, or beyond, your marriage is worth the cost Christ has paid. You don't need to be in a failing marriage to justify marriage counseling. It is meant to strengthen your relationship at any given point in time. A healthy marriage can always use a bit more Jesus too. Why not invest the time, effort, and emotions to ensure the strength of your marriage now?

We know that not every example or point may apply to your marriage journey, but now is the time to put a new stake in the ground from which this next part of your lives will start from. Take what you have learned, worked on, fought for, and leaned into, and write that wisdom upon your hearts.

Testing Your "Ready-Set-Went"

Let's go back to the first day we all met. We "went" on quite a journey with Jesus as we navigated this program together, didn't we? It may seem distant, but you likely remember that we did that seemingly silly Ready-Set-Go exercise before starting all of this to see how well the two of you communicated and worked as one.

Now, let us do the Ready-Set-Go exercise again. This program has not been some infomercial promising a money-back guarantee in the next ten minutes if you do what we say, but we have faith in God that who you were then is not who you are now. What did taking the test now reveal to the both of you? For us, we had quite a few more laughs, but we also enjoyed seeing the progress we had made as we traveled our Emmaus Road with Jesus. We are confident this new "test" has shown you are closer, work better together, communicate more clearly, and love so much deeper. It sure did for us.

A Covenant – Three in One

It may help to approach creating a covenant for yourselves in a similar manner to how you worked to create a SMART goal. Fully defining the scope of your covenant will help you to maintain your focus for fulfilling this covenant you have made to each other and God.

Going forward, we strongly encourage you to create a covenant in which to hold yourselves accountable as you continue your journey, put pen to paper, and then live it out. We pray God's blessing over your journey.

Your Emmaus *Roadmap* to Marriage

A Marriage Discipleship Journey (Worksheet)

| This Roadmap Belongs To: | |

Session 1 – Priorities & Partnership

Preparing the Way – Impact Verses   (What stood out to you?)

_____
_____
_____

Walking with Him – Teaching Points   (Session Discussion Notes)

_____
_____
_____
_____

For the Road – Taking it With You   (Tools & Takeaways for the Road)

_____
_____
_____
_____

Session 2 – Communication & Conflict

Preparing the Way – Impact Verses   (What stood out to you?)

_____
_____
_____
_____

Walking with Him – Teaching Points   (Session Discussion Notes)

_____
_____
_____
_____
_____
_____
_____
_____
_____
_____

For the Road – Taking it With You   (Tools & Takeaways for the Road)

_____
_____
_____
_____

Session 3 – Spirit & Spark

Preparing the Way – Impact Verses   (What stood out to you?)

_____
_____
_____
_____

Walking with Him – Teaching Points   (Session Discussion Notes)

_____
_____
_____
_____
_____
_____
_____
_____
_____
_____

For the Road – Taking it With You   (Tools & Takeaways for the Road)

_____
_____
_____
_____

Session 4 – Faith & Forgiveness

Preparing the Way - Impact Verses   (What stood out to you?)

_____
_____
_____
_____

Walking with Him - Teaching Points   (Session Discussion Notes)

_____
_____
_____
_____
_____
_____
_____
_____
_____

For the Road - Taking it With You   (Tools & Takeaways for the Road)

_____
_____
_____
_____

SESSION 5 – LEADERSHIP & SUPPORT

Preparing the Way – Impact Verses (What stood out to you?)

_____

_____

_____

_____

Walking with Him – Teaching Points (Session Discussion Notes)

_____

_____

_____

_____

_____

_____

_____

_____

_____

_____

For the Road – Taking it With You (Tools & Takeaways for the Road)

_____

_____

_____

_____

Session 6 – Pursuit & Intimacy

Preparing the Way – Impact Verses   (What stood out to you?)

___

Walking with Him – Teaching Points   (Session Discussion Notes)

___

For the Road – Taking it With You   (Tools & Takeaways for the Road)

___

Session 7 – Privacy & Protection

Preparing the Way – Impact Verses   (What stood out to you?)

_____

_____

_____

_____

Walking with Him – Teaching Points   (Session Discussion Notes)

_____

_____

_____

_____

_____

_____

_____

_____

_____

For the Road – Taking it With You   (Tools & Takeaways for the Road)

_____

_____

_____

_____

Session 8 – Modeling & Praise

Preparing the Way – Impact Verses (What stood out to you?)

_____
_____
_____
_____

Walking with Him – Teaching Points (Session Discussion Notes)

_____
_____
_____
_____
_____
_____
_____
_____
_____

For the Road – Taking it With You (Tools & Takeaways for the Road)

_____
_____
_____
_____

Session 9 – Projects & Work

Preparing the Way – Impact Verses   (What stood out to you?)

_____
_____
_____
_____

Walking with Him – Teaching Points   (Session Discussion Notes)

_____
_____
_____
_____
_____
_____
_____
_____
_____
_____

For the Road – Taking it With You   (Tools & Takeaways for the Road)

_____
_____
_____
_____

SESSION 10 – NOW & THEN

Preparing the Way – Impact Verses   (What stood out to you?)

_____
_____
_____
_____

Walking with Him – Teaching Points   (Session Discussion Notes)

_____
_____
_____
_____
_____
_____
_____
_____

For the Road – Taking it With You   (Tools & Takeaways for the Road)

_____
_____
_____
_____

Program Summary – Wisdom For The Road

Next Steps – Knowledge with Action   (Where do we go from here?)

_____
_____
_____
_____

Planning for Success – To-dos for You   (What will we do to get there?)

_____
_____
_____
_____
_____
_____
_____
_____
_____

Our Covenant – To Persevere as One   (A Statement of Commitment with Christ)

_____
_____
_____
_____

Resources & Citations

Chapman, G. D. *The 5 Love Languages: The Secret to Love That Lasts*. (Northfield Publishing, 2024).

De Becker, G. *The Gift of Fear: And Other Survival Signals That Protect Us From Violence*. (Dell Publishing, 1999).

Sinek, S. *Find Your Why*. (Portfolio/Penguin, an imprint of Penguin Random House, LLC., 2017).

Wikipedia. "Active listening." Last modified March 2021. https://en.wikipedia.org/wiki/Active_listening

Wycliffe Bible Translators. "6 Qualities of a Servant Leader." Last modified September 13, 2016. https://www.wycliffe.org/blog/featured/6-qualities-of-a-servant-leader

Supporting Resource Connections

https://5lovelanguages.com/quizzes/love-language

https://5lovelanguages.com/store/the-5-love-languages

Acknowledgments

We want to thank the countless friends and family that have encouraged and supported us in the development of this program we so dearly love. Without their sacrifices and discipleship, this work would not have become a reality. It is our sincere hope that you will take the blessings God has given you and choose to walk alongside another couple seeking a closer relationship with Jesus. We pray that the revelation of Christ's deep love for you through the breaking of the bread while on this journey with Him has blessed you beyond measure. It truly has been our pleasure to walk alongside you on this journey as well, on your **Emmaus Road to Marriage**. Thank you from the bottom of our hearts, and may God continue to bless you from the very depths of His unending love–for *you*.

www.ingramcontent.com/pod-product-compliance
Lightning Source LLC
LaVergne TN
LVHW081543060526
838200LV00048B/2194